Some people in the New Age field write because, like me, they were born with a strong need to write. Others are writing because they want to share their discoveries, experiences, and expertise with others. There is enormous personal satisfaction in contributing to the process in which knowledge is made available to others. I imagine a few people are writing New Age books purely for the money, but they would be rare. Most people writing for this market have knowledge to impart, and in most cases, the financial rewards are not as large as non-writers imagine.

If you have a genuine interest in the New Age and enjoy writing, you will find this a fertile and rewarding field to be in. I hope that this book will help you achieve success in the New Age market, no matter what your motivations are.

—Richard Webster

About the Author

Richard Webster is the author of more than twenty-five books published by Llewellyn Publications during the last decade, as well as many others published in New Zealand and elsewhere. A resident of New Zealand, he travels extensively, giving classes, workshops, and lectures on the topics of which he writes. For many years he conducted *Wake Up and Write!* seminars. Webster has been involved in psychic subjects for most of his life, beginning at the age of nine with a study of palmistry. He joined the Theosophical Society at seventeen

To Write to the Author

If you wish to contact the author or would like more information about this book, please write to the author in care of Llewellyn Worldwide and we will forward your request. Both the author and publisher appreciate hearing from you and learning of your enjoyment of this book and how it has helped you. Llewellyn Worldwide cannot guarantee that every letter written to the author can be answered, but all will be forwarded. Write to:

Richard Webster
℅ Llewellyn Worldwide
P.O. Box 64383, Dept. 0-7387-0344-3
St. Paul, MN 55164-0383, U.S.A.

Please enclose a self-addressed stamped envelope for reply,
or $1.00 to cover costs. If outside U.S.A., enclose
international postal reply coupon.

Many of Llewellyn's authors have websites with additional information
and resources. For more information, please visit our website at
http://www.llewellyn.com.

How to
Write
for the
New Age
Market

Richard Webster

2003
Llewellyn Publications
St. Paul, Minnesota, 55164-0383, U.S.A.

FIRST EDITION
First Printing, 2003

Book interior design and editing by Connie Hill
Cover design by Gavin Dayton Duffy
Cover image © 2002 by Brand X Pictures

Library of Congress Cataloging-in-Publication Data
Webster, Richard
How to write for the new age market / Richard Webster.
p. cm.
Includes bibliographical references and index.
ISBN 0-7387-0344-3
Data pending

Llewellyn Worldwide does not participate in, endorse, or have any authority or responsibility concerning private business transactions between our authors and the public.

All mail addressed to the author is forwarded but the publisher cannot, unless specifically instructed by the author, give out an address or phone number.

Any Internet references contained in this work are current at publication time, but the publisher cannot guarantee that a specific location will continue to be maintained. Please refer to the publisher's website for links to authors' websites and other sources.

Llewellyn Publications
A Division of Llewellyn Worldwide, Ltd.
P.O. Box 64383, Dept. 0-7387-0344-3
St. Paul, MN 55164-0383, U.S.A.
www.llewellyn.com

Printed in the United States of America

For my good friend
Adey Ramsel

| ALSO BY RICHARD WEBSTER

Astral Travel for Beginners

Aura Reading for Beginners

The Complete Book of Palmistry

Dowsing for Beginners

Feng Shui for Beginners

Is Your Pet Psychic?

Llewellyn Feng Shui series

Omens, Oghams & Oracles

Palm Reading for Beginners

Pendulum Magic for Beginners

Playing Card Divination for Beginners

Practical Guide to Past-Life Memories

Seven Secrets to Success

Soul Mates

Spirit Guides and Angel Guardians

Success Secrets

Write Your Own Magic

| Contents

| Acknowledgments

It is hard to acknowledge everyone in a book of this sort. My first book was published more than thirty years ago, and many people have helped me along the road to becoming a full-time writer:

I would like to thank David Mackie, who gave me my first job in publishing, way back in 1964.

Martin Breese became my first British publisher in 1986, and is now one of my best friends.

Everyone at Llewellyn, who gave me my big American opportunity. Not a day goes past when I don't thank you all for the care and attention you pay to my books.

Nancy J. Mostad, acquisitions manager at Llewellyn, took me out for breakfast even before I had a book accepted by Llewellyn. I wouldn't be where I am now without you, Nancy. Thank you for your friendship and enthusiasm.

Graham Little, Colin J. Peel, Adey Ramsel, and Ken Ring, fellow professional writers and good friends.

Ted Andrews, Pat Monaghan, Dorothy Morrison, Jonn Mumford, and Silver RavenWolf—all fellow Llewellyn authors and good friends.

Ann Andrews, Michele Comeau, Lisa Cork, and Morgan Mac-Arthur. I'd hate to think what life would be like without our regular Master Mind sessions.

Shayne and Judelle Thompson.

Alan and Michele Watson.

Margaret, my wife, and our children Nigel, Charlotte, and Philip. Thank you for letting me follow my dream.

And, especially for this book, Ann Kerns at Llewellyn. This book has been her special project, and I am grateful for being given the opportunity to write it. Most of chapter ten is her work. This book is much better and more comprehensive because of her input. Thank you very much, Ann.

FOREWORD

I met Richard Webster for the first time on June 20, 1992, over breakfast at a hotel where he was attending a convention. We talked about his palmistry book, which he hoped Llewellyn would agree to publish. We did contract that book, and many more since then. Richard impressed me with his authenticity, gentle manners, and knowledge of the subject matter. Since that meeting, we have pitched many ideas back and forth to each other and this, *How to Write for the New Age Market*, is Richard's twenty-fifth book with Llewellyn. There are still many Webster projects in the works.

Because of his broad publishing experience, including some years as an editor, and his excellent record as a Llewellyn ambassador at many trade shows around the world, Richard has the knowledge and authority to write this book. When we began discussing the project, Richard mentioned that he had already written and printed a small booklet on the subject of getting published and also did workshops on the subject—thus he already had a framework for the book.

While our writer's guidelines tell new writers what they need to do to submit their work, *How to Write for the New Age Market* tells them why they should follow our guidelines and gives a new writer a glimpse into the world of niche publishing, in this case the New Age market. In addition to useful guidance for book writing in general, the book helps writers understand the reality of niche publishing and dispels mistaken impressions and expectations that many writers have at the onset of their writing careers. It explains the important partnership of publisher and writer and how such a committed partnership can lead to success for both. You will learn how to have a productive and happy relationship with your editor and how to work with your publisher to promote your book. All of these valuable tips come from an expert who is a successful author in the New Age genre, and who is held in high esteem by his publisher, Carl Llewellyn Weschcke, and all the staff at Llewellyn Worldwide, Ltd.

In my sixteen years with Llewellyn, I have attempted to explain the tenets contained in this book to new authors over and over again, because Llewellyn encourages new authors to submit manuscripts. *How to Write for the New Age Market* is the one source for answers to getting published in this niche and a method of "customer service" for new writer's hoping to receive a publication agreement from Llewellyn. While the staff is still here to answer questions, we hope this book will give you the confidence and encouragement to submit your ideas and proposals.

Nancy J. Mostad
Acquisitions Manager
Llewellyn Worldwide, Ltd.

Introduction

The "New Age" is a convenient term to describe the rapid growth of mystical and psychic awareness that spread around the world in the late 1960s, and has continued to grow, expand, and develop ever since. Although it is generally associated with an interest in psychic phenomena, the New Age is much broader than that. It encompasses a wide range of beliefs and has higher consciousness, expanded awareness, and enlightenment as its goals. The New Age is not a religion or movement. In fact, people from many different cultures and religions profess to be New-Agers. It has no central organization or hierarchical structure. Every person in the New Age is free to find his or her own path to self-realization. The one belief that most New-agers share is that we all need to work together to create a more enlightened world where everybody can be free, and lead good, healthy, peaceful lives.

In a sense, there has always been a "new age." There is even mention of it in the Bible: "And I saw a new heaven and a new earth: for the first heaven and the first earth were passed away" (Revelation 21:1). The esoteric tradition has continued throughout history, despite frequent repression and persecution. Shamans, and other people with special powers, passed on their hidden knowledge to enable the tradition to continue. Joachim of Fiore, Emmanuel Swedenborg, Madame Helena Blavatsky, Annie Besant, Rudolf Steiner, Alice Bailey, Edgar Cayce, and many others all helped pave the way to the current New Age.

The New Age has gone mainstream. You are likely to find free New Age newspapers near the exit doors at your local supermarket. Books in this field are prominently displayed in bookstores everywhere—in the past you had to seek them out in specialist occult bookstores. Hollywood has discovered the New Age and produced many films to cash in on the public's interest. Programs such as *The X-Files* on television help promote interest in the New Age. Psychic readers and psychic fairs can be found everywhere. Adult education classes in astrology, channeling, meditation, dream interpretation, yoga, tai chi, tarot, feng shui, aura reading, and past life regression are just some of the courses readily available, even in small towns. The holistic health movement is steadily gaining in strength. Alternative religions, such as Buddhism, Hinduism, and Taoism are gaining converts at the expense of traditional Western religions. Wicca can now be talked about openly, and books on the subject can be found in almost any bookstore.

The New Age is a misleading term, as most New Age beliefs are extremely old. However, fortunately for New Age writers, the New Age is enjoying a renaissance. Some people say that the increased growth in spiritual awareness occurred when the Age of Aquarius began, arguably in the late 1960s. In fact, it probably began a century earlier with the growth of Theosophy and New Thought. Whatever the cause, growth has been rapid. In 1987 a survey by the National Opinion Research Council revealed that 67 percent of all American adults believed that they had experienced some form of psychic phenomena. Forty-two percent believed they had contacted the dead, and 31 percent had experienced clairvoyance.[1]

The New Age offers tremendous opportunities for writers. The June 1987 issue of *Forbes* magazine reported that the New Age market was worth 3.43 billion dollars annually. There are more publishers specializing in this market than ever before, and they are constantly looking for authors who can write powerful books for their readers. Consequently, in this field, beginning authors are welcomed and encouraged.[2] The New Age is also one of the few areas of publishing where an agent is not essential.

The subjects that New Age authors can write about is incredibly diverse. A small selection of potential topics includes:

Akashic records	Gnosticism	psychic phenomena
alchemy	hypnotism	psychokinesis
alternative healing	incense	psychometry
angels	intuition	Qabala
Arthurian tradition	iridology	radiesthesia
astral travel	Jainism	reincarnation
astrology	karma	self-transformation
auras	lightworking	spirituality
bodywork	magick	tarot
Buddhism	meditation	Theosophy
candles	metaphysics	UFOs
chakras	mythology	voodoo
channeling	Native American	Wicca
clairvoyance	spirituality	women's spirituality
crystals	numerology	xenoglossia
dowsing	omens	yoga
dreams	palmistry	Zen Buddhism
Eastern teachings	precognition	
feng shui	psi	

This quick run through the alphabet shows that you need never run out of subjects to write about.

Naturally, you must have a strong interest in the New Age if you intend writing for this market. You have to enjoy reading and studying New Age books. I would never consider writing romance novels, for instance, as I have no desire to read them. I know several successful romance writers, and admire what they do. They are all voracious readers of romance novels. It is essential that you read a large number of New Age books before thinking about writing for this market.

People who read New Age books are often extremely knowledgeable and will be quick to let you know of any errors you make.

You also need to be persistent, dedicated, motivated, willing to research, and prepared to learn and take advice. Your age has no bearing on your chances of being published. Neither does your sex, politics, race, nationality, or educational level. If you have the necessary knowledge and are able to express yourself well with words on paper, you can become a successful New Age author.

People write books for many different reasons. They may want to entertain or inform others. There may be a desire for the prestige and recognition that comes from having a book published. Some people write because they see it as a path to wealth and fame. For others, a book enables them to advance in their careers. A few may even write to achieve a form of immortality with their prose, hoping that, after their death, their writing will still live on.

I became a writer because I was born with a strong need to write. I express myself best with words on paper. At the age of ten I was producing a small newspaper that I sold to my neighbors. I also wrote short stories for the children's page of the local newspaper.

When I left school I went into publishing, thinking that this would give me the necessary inside knowledge to become a successful author. What I learned was invaluable. In my seven years in publishing I spent time working in the production, editorial, marketing, and sales departments, and finally became an editor. However, my time in publishing almost put me off writing forever. One of my early jobs was working out the royalty statements for authors and I was horrified at how little most of them earned. I should have taken heart from the significant incomes enjoyed by the best-selling authors, but instead I temporarily put my dream on hold.

When I left publishing, I bought a bookstore, and later became the New Zealand agent for several American publishers. Consequently, I have experienced a variety of roles in the book business.

I have also worked as a professional psychic. I have made my living as a palmist in several different countries. For several years I conducted horoscope parties in people's homes. I then began teaching psychic development classes. I started these in my own home, but they became so popular that I had to move them to a local community center. I learned a great deal from these experiences, and they have formed the basis of many of my books.

My first book came out in 1972, and was an example of beginner's luck. The first publisher I sent it to accepted it, and must have had enormous faith in the project as he printed just five hundred copies. However, it was a start. Over the years, more than seventy-five of my books have been published, and I am finally fulfilling my childhood dream of being a full-time writer.

For some years I conducted *Wake Up and Write!* seminars, which were intended to motivate the many people who were daydreaming about writing, but were not doing anything about it. I hope some of that motivation will come across in this book.

Most of my books have been in the New Age category. However, I have also written three novels, and ghost-wrote twenty books on a wide variety of subjects for other people. As a result of that experience, I wrote a book called *Secrets of Ghost Writing*.[3]

Some people in the New Age field are writing because, like me, they *have* to write. Others are writing because they want to share their discoveries, experiences, and expertise with others. These people, who are usually experts in a particular field, might write only one or two books, but their knowledge and wisdom is invaluable for all of us, and we are fortunate that they choose to write their thoughts down. There is enormous personal satisfaction in contributing to the process in which knowledge is made available to others. I imagine a few people are writing New Age books purely for the money, but they would be rare. Most people writing for this market have knowledge to impart, and in most cases, the financial rewards are not as large as nonwriters imagine.

I hope this book will help you achieve success in the New Age market, no matter what your motivations are. I have more than twenty years of experience in writing in this field. I have made every mistake that it is possible to make, and hope that this book will enable you to avoid many of them.

If you have a genuine interest in the New Age and enjoy writing, you will find this a fertile and rewarding field to be in. It is unlikely that you will become a household name or that your books will appear on *The New York Times* bestseller lists, but you can make a comfortable living writing in this field, and will be able to help an enormous number of people in the process. The sense of excitement you will experience when you realize that your knowledge and writing are helping other people to achieve their goals is indescribable.

Finally, writing a book is a voyage of self-discovery. Whether your book is published or not, you will learn a great deal about yourself.

1

BEFORE YOU START

Most nonwriters think that authors come up with an idea and then sit down and write a book. Life would be easy for writers if this was the case. In fact, coming up with a good idea is just the starting point. Nonwriters have no idea of the amount of thought and work that needs to take place before the author even starts writing his or her book.

| CHOOSING A TOPIC

You probably already know what the subject of your New Age book is going to be. Perhaps your specialized knowledge of a particular subject has created the motivation to write a certain book. You already know a great deal about your subject and want to express your thoughts on paper.

You may have experienced something that you want to impart to others. Betty J. Eadie is a good example of an author who did just that. According to her book, *Embraced by the Light*, she died after an operation and returned to life four hours later, with amazing insights about life on the other side. Her book was on the *New York Times* best-seller list for more than forty weeks, and occupied the number-one spot for five weeks. The paperback rights were sold to Bantam Books for one and a half million dollars. The sequel, *The Awakening Heart: My Continuing Journey to Love*, was published in 1996 by Pocket Books. The first print run was one million copies.[1]

My first book for Llewellyn was on palmistry. This was a deliberate choice on my part. I had become reasonably well-known as a palmist, and had appeared many times on radio and television to talk about the subject. I had also put out a palmistry video.[2] Consequently, it made sense for me to finally sit down and write a book on the subject.

However, it is also possible that you want to write a New Age book, but as yet are not clear on what aspect of the New Age you want to write about. In this case, you need to spend time thinking about the topics you are interested in. You probably know more about these subjects than you think you do. When you are interested in a particular topic you gain information about it almost by osmosis.

It is important that the topic of your book excites you. You are going to be totally immersed in this subject for a long time. When I worked as a ghostwriter, I wrote books that interested the person who was paying me, but did not excite me. Some of them were monumentally boring, and I used to worry that if I, as the writer, was bored, surely the reader would feel the same. When I gave up ghost-writing I resolved to write books only on topics that intrigued, excited, and stimulated me. Writing about something that excites you is still hard work, but the work seems like play. Writing about something that does not interest you is plain hard work. Fortunately, the New Age encompasses a large variety of subjects, and you will never run out of exciting topics to write on.

... the fact that you are not yet an authority does not mean that you should not write the book ...

The best topic for a book is one that excites not only you, but also your publisher and the audience it is written for. An excited publisher will do an excellent job at publishing and promoting the book, and an excited audience will buy many thousands of copies.

Your own reading and research will frequently provide you with ideas about a book you could write. Have you ever read something and afterward thought that you could write a much better book on that subject? Are there gaps in the books you read that you could fill? Maybe a book you read contains errors of fact or omission. You could write a book providing a more honest and accurate account of the subject.

In every field there are good, average, mediocre, and bad books. Find the worst book you can find on a subject and make a list of the reasons why you think it is so bad. Evaluate this list and write a paragraph or two on a proposed book you could write on this subject that would provide a reader with everything that he or she would need to know. Do the same with the very best book you can find on the same subject, listing the reasons it is so good. See if you can come up with ideas to write an even better book than the very best book that is already available.

Browse through bookstores and look at books that have already been published on the subject you intend writing about. Look at the subtitles to see what the author of each book is focusing on. Naturally, your book will need to have a different approach to the subject.

| Fiction or Nonfiction

There is a small market for good New Age fiction. However, there is a huge market for good New Age nonfiction. Publishers are more likely to publish a New Age nonfiction book by an unknown author than a novel by the same person. Nonfiction usually sells better than fiction, and continues selling, frequently for many years. Novels usually have a short life. Finally, in difficult times, people buy more nonfiction than fiction. According to an article in the *Wall Street Journal* (July 18, 2001), fiction sales decline when the economy is declining. However, nonfiction sales increase. When times are hard, people seek out valuable information from nonfiction books, but are prepared to defer purchase of a novel, which is read for entertainment.

My recommendation is that you focus on nonfiction. Of course, there are always exceptions. *The Celestine Prophecy* by James Redfield was on the *New York Times* best-seller list for 165 weeks, and was the best-selling book of 1996. Redfield couldn't find a publisher for this book, and eventually published it himself. He sold 150,000 copies himself before selling the rights to Warner Books for a reputed $800,000.[3] Consequently, I would never advise you not to write fiction. However, most New Age writers are more likely to achieve success with their nonfiction than their fiction.

| WHAT TYPE OF NONFICTION SHOULD YOU WRITE?

The easy answer to this is to write the sort of nonfiction that you like to read. However, the type of nonfiction you write will largely be determined by the publisher you choose. Llewellyn publishes how-to books and practical reference books. If you write a good how-to book on an aspect of the New Age that is exciting to you, there is a good possibility that they will publish it. However, they would not be interested in a channeled book from an entity on another planet, as Llewellyn does not publish that type of book.

How-to books are always popular as people want to learn new and different skills. *Dowsing for Beginners* (Llewellyn, 1996) is an example of a how-to book. Self-help books fall into the same general area. Self-help books pinpoint a problem, and then come up with strategies to resolve it. My book *Seven Secrets to Success* (Llewellyn, 1997) is a self-help book.

There is always a need for practical reference books. These books usually do not sell large quantities initially, but can keep on selling for many years. The contribution that the authors of this type of book make to the New Age field is incalculable. *The Magician's Companion* by Bill Whitcomb and the two-volume *The Key of It All* by David Allen Hulse (Llewellyn, both published in 1993) are good examples of this type of book.

There is a smaller market for books that discuss New Age topics, but are not practical, how-to books. A book on the history of the Golden Dawn would fit into this category, but it would not be as popular as a book that taught the secret rituals of the Golden Dawn.

Channeled books are a separate category again. There are a number of specialist publishers who are interested in this type of book, but they are hard to sell. Most channeled books are self-published.

| Are You Qualified to Write This Book?

Naturally, you must have some interest in a subject to even contemplate writing a complete book on it, but you certainly do not need to be an expert at the start. However, you should be an expert by the time you have finished writing it. Every book requires research. If you are already an expert on the subject, your book will require little research. If you know much less, you will have to do extensive research. I enjoy the writing more than any other aspect of creating a book. Consequently, I prefer to write books on subjects that I already know a reasonable amount about.

You can become an expert in any subject if you are prepared to work and study at it. Consequently, the fact that you are not yet an authority does not mean that you should not write the book. Every day journalists write articles on topics that they are not necessarily experts on. However, they find the facts, interview the right people, and create informative articles. You can do exactly the same with your book.

You have to know more about the subject than you intend including in your book. This additional knowledge will give you a sense of authority, which will be picked up subliminally by your readers. Conversely, your readers will also sense when you are struggling with the subject.

This expertise needs to be practical as well as theoretical. If you intend writing a book on palmistry, for instance, you will have to read hundreds of palms before starting to write. I feel that practical experience is just as important as the theoretical. How can you teach someone how to astral travel, for instance, if you have never visited the astral plane yourself?

| IS THERE A NEED FOR YOUR BOOK?

Some 60,000 new books are published every year, and you would imagine that there is a market for a book on virtually any subject. However, this is not necessarily the case.

About thirty years ago, when I was in India, I learned how to construct and interpret numerological yantras. Yantras fascinate me and I thought they would make a wonderful topic for a book. I finally wrote the book (*Talisman Magic*, Llewellyn, 1995), and quickly discovered that not many people in the West share my enthusiasm for yantras. Although the book sold reasonably well, it did not sell as many copies as I had hoped. I thought that writing the first book in the West on this important topic would guarantee its success. However, most people had no idea what a yantra was, and were not prepared to hand over their hard-earned cash to find out.

The first book I wrote for Llewellyn was a book on palmistry (*Revealing Hands*, Llewellyn, 1994). I have more than four hundred books on palmistry in my own library, and more books appear on the subject every year. At first glance it appears ridiculous to write yet another book on a subject that has already been covered so comprehensively. However, the reason there are so many books available on palmistry is because a large number of people are interested in the subject, and want to learn more about it.

Consequently, before you write a single word, you should find out how many books are already available on the topic you intend writing about. This is a simple task now, as a quick search on Amazon.com will list all the books that are currently in print on your subject, as well as many that are out of print. Bookfinder.com lists many out-of-print titles that are available from used bookstores.

As well as going on the Internet, I also visit New Age bookstores and libraries to have a look at any books on the subject that I am not already familiar with. I want to see how the information is presented, the number and type of illustrations, and what original contributions I can make to justify the publication of another book on this particular subject.

You might find that there are no books on the subject on which you intend to write. In this case, you should do some serious thinking before proceeding further. It is possible that there is no book on this topic because no one is interested enough in the subject to buy a book on it. However, the opposite might also apply. You may have discovered something that will start a whole new trend.

You are more likely to find hundreds of books on your area of interest. There is no point in simply writing yet another book on a subject, unless you have something new to offer. In *Revealing Hands*, I included a chapter on my researches into dermatoglyphics. This information had never been in print anywhere before, and became a major point of difference. *Revealing Hands* has now been reprinted as *The Complete Book of Palmistry*. For this new edition, I wrote a chapter on Indian thumb reading. Again, this is information that has not previously been published in the West. You may not have any new information, but instead have a new way of presenting it that makes the topic easier to understand. This, also, becomes a point of difference.

Naturally, a publisher has to make money to stay in business. Your book may contain fascinating information, but if the publisher is able to sell only a few hundred copies, he will lose money if he publishes it. Consequently, while looking at books on the same or similar topics to the one you are planning to write, check to see how many times they have been reprinted. Did you find any of them on the remainder table? In the case of library books, you may be able to see how many times they have been borrowed. You can also see how popular different books are by checking their rankings on sites like Amazon.com and Barnesandnoble.com.

It is a good idea to think like a publisher when estimating the need for a book. If you were a publisher and received the manuscript you intend writing, would you be excited?

| WHO ARE YOU WRITING FOR?

Most beginning writers say that they are writing for a general audience. They feel that their topic is so important that everyone will want to read it. Sadly, this is not the case. Newspapers and general interest magazines are written for a general audience, but most other writing has to be targeted to a specific market. Fortunately, this makes the writing task easier, as you can keep a picture of your target reader in your mind as you write.

It is important to think about your potential audience before starting to write. Who are you writing your book for? Sometimes the answer is obvious. If you are planning to write a book on Sabian symbols your market is going to be serious astrologers. Consequently, you will not need to explain many of the technical terms that appear in your book. However, your approach would change dramatically if you decided to write a book on Sabian symbols for people who had no prior knowledge of astrology. In this case, you would need to devote much of the book to an explanation of the basics of astrology, and the meanings of all the terms. Your whole approach to the book would be completely different.

Many years ago, I read somewhere that Malcolm Forbes published *Forbes* magazine for a dentist in Des Moines. I remember this well, as it showed an incredible understanding of his market. If a dentist in Des Moines enjoyed each issue of *Forbes*, so would everyone else in his target market. Consequently, each issue was designed to appeal to this imaginary person.

I write my books in the same way. I always have someone in mind whenever I write. Most of the time, this is an imaginary person. I do not necessarily use the same person each time, because so much depends on the particular book I am writing.

My first book, *Freedom to Read* (HPP Press, 1972), was a study of censorship. I no longer recall who my imaginary reader was for this book, but can guarantee that it was not the same person I had in mind while writing *Success Secrets* or *Aura Reading for Beginners*. I have an imaginary person in mind while writing this book. I visualize someone who is intelligent, sincere, eager to learn, knowledgeable about some aspects of the New Age, prepared to work hard, and keen to become a successful, published author. My last book was written for an imaginary sixteen-year-old girl.

Your choice of imaginary reader will determine how you write your book. Will you write in a chatty manner? Or would it be better to write your book in a more authoritative way? The slant you take, the words you use, and even the length of individual sentences, paragraphs, and chapters will be determined by the maturity and educational level of your imaginary reader.

Choose an intelligent person. Your readers will quickly know if you are condescending and talking down to them. A good choice is to choose someone who has a great deal of common sense, but is not familiar with the subject you are writing about. I make sure that all of my imaginary people are friendly, discerning, intelligent, and possess a good sense of humor.

The choice of reader will also ultimately determine the sales potential of the book. A book written with a teenage girl in mind is probably going to be an introductory book to a particular subject. You would write a popular, rather than a scholarly, book to appeal to this person. This means that, ideally, it will have a much wider appeal than a book written for a middle-aged academic. There is nothing wrong in writing books for mature academics, but by doing this you are probably limiting the size of your potential market, which in turn limits sales, and that naturally reduces your royalties.

It is not easy to find the right voice, but it is an important part of the writing process. Fortunately, you can change your imaginary reader if you find he or she is not right for the particular book you are working on. If I discover this at, say, chapter four, I do not return to the start and rewrite the book. I simply make a note to remind myself of what I have done, and change anything necessary when revising the book.

| Why Are You Writing This Book?

There are many reasons why people decide to write books, and you should have a clear idea of your motivations before starting work. It takes a huge amount of time and effort to write a book, and you need to keep your goals clearly in mind as you write. If you don't, the chances are that you will never finish the book.

Here are some of the more common reasons why people write books. You might find your motivations in this list:

1. To make money.

2. To teach others.

3. To position yourself in the marketplace as an expert on a particular subject.

4. To become more visible in your field.

5. Because you love writing.

6. To have a book to sell after giving lectures and presentations.

It is important that your goals are realistic and attainable. It is not realistic to expect to make a million dollars from your first book, for instance. It is possible, of course, and a few fortunate authors have done it. However, most authors do not make a full-time living from their writing. They work in all sorts of different fields, and the money they make from writing enables them to enjoy a more comfortable lifestyle than would otherwise be the case.

Evaluate your goals carefully. Some years ago someone told me that he wanted to write a book to impress his mother-in-law. I told him there were much better ways to make his mother-in-law proud of him.

| Are You Holding Yourself Back?

I am always meeting people who say they want to write a book, but somehow never get around to doing it. There is always something that prevents them from writing. There are a number of fears that hold people back.

1. Fear of failure is the most common. Every successful author has experienced failure at one time or another. Every time a book or article is rejected, the author, no matter how experienced he or she is, experiences failure. Most authors experience self-doubt along the way as well.

2. Fear of success. Many would-be authors start their books, but never finish them. As long as the book is not finished, they run no risk of being successful. An acquaintance of mine has been working on a book on Nostradamus for at least twenty years. I doubt if he will ever finish it.

3. Fear of criticism. No one likes to be criticized, but it is a fact of life for writers. Not everyone is going to love your book. The critics may not be kind, and some of your readers will not enjoy reading it.

4. Fear of having nothing to say. This is a particularly insidious fear that makes people feel worthless and insignificant. If nothing you write has any value, why would you even attempt to put words down on paper?

If fears like these are holding you back, examine them carefully, because you have to eliminate them before you can start a writing career. In the cold light of day, these fears seem ridiculous, but they have the power to prevent you from embarking on a satisfying and worthwhile career. The best remedy for fears of this sort is to totally forget any thoughts of publication, and to write the book for your own pleasure and satisfaction. Once the book is written, you can look at it again and decide what to do with it.

| THE TITLE

It is a good idea to have a tentative title in mind before starting to write the book. This helps you focus your thoughts on the exact topic of the book. Ideally, you want a strong, saleable title that is memorable and says exactly what the book is about. *Think and Grow Rich* (The Ralston Society, Meriden, Conn., 1937) is an excellent example. It is short, memorable, and says everything that the potential reader needs to know.

It takes time and effort to come up with a good title. However, this time is well spent, as a good title will help make your book a success. Write down everything that occurs to you, and see how many different titles you can come up with. You will be surprised at the number of titles you can create in a brainstorming session.

Choose the best and use that as your working title. Other ideas will occur to you as you write the book. Add these to your list, because you might decide to change the title before sending the book to your publisher.

Cute titles often confuse potential readers. It might be better to call your book "How to Read Auras" rather than "Swirling Vistas of Color." The first title may not be exciting, but it tells the reader exactly what the book is about. The second title could be almost anything. Fortunately, you can add a subtitle to explain what the book is about. If you were positive that "Swirling Vistas of Color" was the best title for your book on auras, "How to Read Auras" would make a good subtitle.

Publishers have the right to change the title, if they wish. After all, they are investing a large sum of money in your book, and naturally want to receive a return on that investment. You can complain if you feel the title your publisher has come up with is not the right one for your book. However, you will need a good argument, as your publisher knows the market much better than you do, and wants a title that the public will respond to.

| INITIAL SYNOPSIS

You have chosen a subject and have discovered that there is a need for the book you intend to write. You have a potential reader in mind. You even have a possible title. Now it is time to write a brief synopsis. This is simply a list of what you intend to include in your book. Consequently, it will probably consist of suggested chapter headings and perhaps a few notes about what each chapter might contain. It is a simple matter to compile a list of chapter headings. All you need do is write down all the interesting things that you can think of about your topic.

At this stage you can also decide what you intend to include in your book, and what material will be left out. When I was in my early twenties, I spent time in India and filled up several notebooks with observations about the minor lines that are found on the palms of the hand. I have enough material for a complete book on the subject. When I was writing *Revealing Hands*, I made a conscious decision not to include any of this material, as it is of minor importance compared to the information that was included in that book. I would have had to devote at least seventy or eighty pages to the minor lines and this would have made the book unbalanced. It was better to keep this information back and include it in a more advanced book on palmistry that I might write one day.

The purpose of this synopsis is to give you some idea about the shape of the book. It will probably change many times as you continue to think about the book you are going to write.

The synopsis also tells you if you have enough material for a complete book. If you are struggling to find ten to fifteen chapter headings, you may have to reconsider your choice of topic. Of course, the opposite situation can also apply. You may find that you have enough material for more than one book on the subject.

I usually start a synopsis by writing down thoughts and ideas on file cards. I do not evaluate these in any way. I simply jot down any ideas that occur to me. I keep the file cards in a box, along with anything else that might prove useful later on when I am writing the book. This could include magazine articles, titles of books, lists of people I should talk to, and so on. I keep on doing this until I decide to write the book. I then dump everything onto the kitchen table and sort them into piles, which gives me the first clues as to possible chapters.

I have been interested in candle magic for many years, but had not thought about writing a book on the subject until recently. In 2001, I was the keynote speaker at a breakfast at the International New Age Trade Show in Denver. I hadn't planned to mention it, but in the course of my talk explained how candle magic had helped my own career. Afterward, several people asked me when my book on candle magic would be coming out. A day or two later, I had lunch with a friend, and the subject came up again. I grabbed a napkin and jotted down a list of possible chapter headings:

1. Introduction—history of candle burning and my own introduction to the subject.

2. What is candle magic?

3. Types of candles.

4. Color.

5. Fragrance.

6. How to dress a candle.

7. Timing—days of the week, planetary hours.

8. Numerology and candles.

9. Magical alphabets—inscribing candles.

10. Magic squares.

11. Healing with candles.

12. Candle rituals—achieving goals, past lives, contacting angels and guides.

This list tells me that I have enough interesting information to consider writing the book. If I had not been able to think of at least ten chapter headings, I would have reconsidered the idea. In that case, I would possibly consider writing a magazine article, rather than a book. Perhaps I could do some more research, and then look at the idea again.

It is an interesting exercise to create brief synopses of as many different subjects as possible. I do this whenever I come across an idea for a potential book. I have a collection of synopses written on paper napkins, old envelopes, the backs of receipts, and on scraps of paper. Do not throw away any of your synopses. File them away, as one day you might decide to write the book.

Synopses can also provide ideas for books. You might write a brief synopsis one day and then forget about it for ten years. When you go through your files, the idea will come back to you, and you might decide to write the book. Alternatively, it might start you thinking about the subject, so that you come up with a fresh approach or a different slant to the topic.

Erle Stanley Gardner, the best-selling mystery writer, never threw away anything. A collection of thirty-six million items belonging to him is now housed at the Humanities Research Center Library at the University of Texas, Austin.[4] I'm not suggesting that you keep everything. However, you will find it useful to file away the synopses of any book ideas that interest you for future reference.

| READ, READ, READ

As you are intending to write books and articles for the New Age market, you should read as many books as possible in this field. Naturally, you will focus mainly on books that are related to the topics you intend writing about, but you should read a variety of other books as well.

Something I found extremely useful when I started was to read as many "how-to" books as possible. You may think that a book on how to repair antique furniture has nothing to do with what you intend writing. Certainly, the subject has no bearing on your proposed books. However, this author has successfully written a book that teaches people how to do something. That is the type of book you are likely to be writing. A large percentage of New Age books fit comfortably into the "how-to" category. Consequently, study as many of these books as you can to see how the author has structured them, and how he or she wrote them.

Finally, read some good fiction. You may feel that this is a waste of time, but you will become a better writer if you read well-written books. This will enable you to write enjoyable books, and your readers will eagerly wait for your next book.

I regularly meet people who want to write, but do not read themselves. I can not see how anyone can become a successful writer without reading and studying the works of others. Read, read, and then read some more. Your writing will benefit enormously as a result.

| BE THE BEST AUTHOR YOU CAN

Naturally, you have to produce the very best book that you are capable of writing on your subject, but there is much more to being an author than sitting down and writing. You will be working with a large number of people as your book gets written, assessed, edited, published, and put on sale. Make sure that at every stage you are as easy to work with as possible. This does not mean that you should meekly acquiesce every time someone asks you to change something. Naturally, you need to insist on what you think is right, but do so in a pleasant, agreeable manner.

Every publishing house has its share of "high maintenance" authors. These are authors who react aggressively every time something occurs that they do not agree with. I have heard astonishing stories of the abuse and foul language that some authors use when dealing with staff members who are doing their best to create a good book. No matter what happens, think first before opening your mouth or putting pen to paper.

Ask about anything you do not understand. The staff in a publishing company do a huge amount of work that you, as an author, never get to hear about. All of this knowledge and expertise is being utilized every day for your benefit, as well as that of your publisher's other authors. The people you deal with will be enthusiastic about your work, and will want your book to be successful. Your success is very much their success, too. Be as pleasant and cooperative as possible. Express your gratitude and thanks to the people who help you. By doing this, you will become an author who everyone enjoys dealing with, and any problems that arise will be dealt with speedily and effectively.

| WHERE AND WHEN WILL YOU WRITE?

You probably will not have a great deal of choice in these matters, at least when you start. Ideally, it would be wonderful to have a separate room that is reserved purely for your writing. However, the kitchen table may have to suffice, and many authors write their books here.

Writing involves a certain amount of discipline. You might have to force yourself to sit down to write initially, but soon the writing will become a habit. If you force yourself to sit down at the same time every day to think and write, you will find yourself doing it automatically after a few weeks.

When you write will probably be dictated by the other members of your household. The best time is when you have few distractions. You may write in the evenings once the children have gone to bed. You might grab an hour while they are at school. I start writing at eight in the morning. This is the best time for me, as the rest of the family have left for work, and the house is quiet.

| DO YOU NEED AN AGENT?

The answer to this question depends on you. You do not need an agent to become a successful New Age author. Ninety percent of Llewellyn's titles are from unagented authors. At Samuel Weiser, 98 percent of their titles are from unagented authors. The percentage is 75 percent at Crossing Press. However, at Celestial Arts only 10 percent of their books come from unagented authors.[5] I know a large number of writers in this field who have never had an agent, and have no intention of using one in the near future. I also know other New Age writers who do have agents and would not consider writing a book without their agent's input.

An agent acts on your behalf through the publishing process. He or she is involved in contract negotiations, and also should be a business advisor, mentor, and friend. An agent can offer advice on preparing book proposals and suitable topics to write on. He or she will gently guide your career to your mutual advantage.

A good agent will leave you free to write your books, while he or she finds the best publishing house and the best possible deal for you. In some ways an author-agent relationship is a partnership, and it will only work if you relate well to your agent and can communicate openly with him or her.

It is not easy to find a good agent. When I was starting out I was unable to find an agent who was willing to represent me. Fortunately, I enjoy the financial aspects of my book-writing business, and feel that I do a reasonable job of it without an agent. I would miss that side of my business if I decided to use an agent.

However, not everyone enjoys the business aspect of a writing career. If you feel that you need an agent, choose him or her carefully. Ideally, you want a long-term relationship with someone who will ultimately become a friend.

There are many ways to find an agent. Ask writer friends if they can recommend anyone. Look at the acknowledgments in as many New Age books as possible to see which agents have been thanked. Ask questions in writers' chat rooms and newsgroups on the Internet. Go through the lists of agents in *Literary Marketplace* and *Guide to Literary Agents* to find agents that work in the New Age field. Prepare a query letter and send it to all the agents who sound suitable. You should receive a positive response from some of them. Ask questions to determine the one who is likely to be best for you.

Here are some questions you should ask:

1. How many New Age books have you sold over the last year? The agent may sell a hundred books a year, but may not have been successful in placing any New Age titles.

2. How long have you been in business? If the agent has been in business for a number of years, he or she is likely to have sold many books and have valuable contacts in the publishing industry.

3. Do you belong to the Association of Authors' Representatives? Members of AAR need to demonstrate that they are ethical and have made sales before being allowed to join. Not every ethical agent belongs, but it is a positive indication of their professionalism if they do.

4. Do you charge upfront fees, such as reading fees or evaluation fees? This is a controversial area as some agents make most of their money from these reading fees. Members of the AAR are not allowed to charge a reading or evaluation fee. Of course, some agents will ask you to reimburse them for any expenses

incurred in selling your book. Photocopying and postage are two examples. These expenses are deducted from your commission, and are not paid upfront.

5. What are your commission rates? It is usually 15 percent for local sales, and 20–25 percent for foreign rights. The higher fee for foreign rights is because the commission is shared with the overseas co-agents.

6. Will you provide me with the contact details of a few of your existing clients? An ethical agent will be happy to give you the names of some authors. Contact them to see if they are happy with the service the agent is providing. Proceed with caution if any of them express doubts about the agent. This is because it is much better to work without an agent, than it is to have a bad one.

7. What happens if you or I terminate the author-agent agreement? Usually, the agent will continue to handle the contracts that have been made, and will continue to receive commissions that he or she is entitled to. However, the agent should not have any claim on anything that is sold after the termination date.

You may feel grateful securing any agent. Think carefully before entering any long-term agreement. It is a business decision like any other, and you need to feel totally comfortable with the agent you choose.

You have made a start. You have chosen a topic, looked at the market, decided there is room for your book, come up with a title, and written a brief synopsis. While doing this you may have had second thoughts about the entire process. Writing a book takes discipline, time, and effort. It can be a daunting task. In the next chapter we will look at two activities that I have found helpful, and that will probably benefit you as well.

2
LITTLE KNOWN SECRETS

Two things have helped me enormously in my own writing career: modeling other writers and being part of a Master Mind group.

MODELING

We all subconsciously model ourselves on others. As children, we watched what our parents and friends did and modeled our actions and behavior on them. As adults, we model ourselves so that we can conform and fit in with whatever group we happen to be in at the time.

This is entirely subconscious. We can be different personalities in different situations. If you take up a new interest and join a group of like-minded people, you will probably be quiet and reserved, at least for a while. You will realize that you may not know as much as some of the others, and will listen more and talk less. However, if the situation is the other way around, and you are the expert, you will probably feel more confident and outgoing, as you are in charge of the situation.

Although you remain the same person, you are exhibiting two different personalities. In fact, there is no limit to the number of personalities you can be. I belong to a number of organizations and am aware that I am a different person at SWAP (Salespeople With A Purpose) Club meetings than I am at Kiwanis Club meetings. Why? Because I subconsciously model myself on the group I happen to be with at the time.

Although we are doing this subconsciously, we can also do it consciously as well. We can watch someone who is already doing what we want to do, and repeat what that person has done. By modeling ourselves in that way, we can avoid some of the mistakes, and concentrate on the things that work. Role models can be an enormous help to us in achieving success.

I first became aware of conscious modeling more than twenty years ago. I found a book called *Bunker Bean* by Harry Leon Wilson in a second-hand bookstore. This book was first published in 1913 and became extremely successful. A few years later, it appeared on Broadway as a stage play called *His Majesty, Bunker Bean*. The play was filmed twice, once in the days of silent movies, and again in 1936, starring a very young Lucille Ball. Although the book has been out of print for many years, motivational speakers regularly tell the story of Bunker Bean. Funnily enough, although it is a work of fiction, most of them seem to think it is a true story.

Bunker Bean grew up thinking that he was a complete failure, someone who was inferior to everyone else. He was a timid, fearful child who became a timid, fearful adult who failed at everything.

One day he visited a fortuneteller who told him that he was the reincarnation of Napoleon Bonaparte. Bunker Bean could not believe it. Here he was, living in poverty, scared of everything, but yet in a previous life he had ruled a large part of the world. He had been rich, brave, and afraid of nothing. The fortuneteller told Bunker that he still contained all of the qualities of Napoleon and the time was right for him to manifest them in his current life.

Bunker was amazed. He went to the library and read everything he could find about Napoleon. He collected pictures of Napoleon and displayed them in his dingy apartment. He began to imitate the speech, manners, and behavioral patterns of Napoleon. In a short period of time, Bunker Bean climbed to the top, both in business and socially. He became rich, powerful, and famous.

One day, he discovered that the fortuneteller was a charlatan, and that she had deceived him. He wasn't the reincarnation of Napoleon, after all. Bunker Bean was devastated, but in the years he had been modeling himself on Napoleon he had acquired the habits that led to success. Being successful was now just as natural to him as being a failure had been before. Bunker Bean decided that every person has the potential to achieve success.

| JACK LONDON

A few years after reading *Bunker Bean* I visited Jack London's home in the wine country north of San Francisco. Jack London had been one of my favorite authors while I was growing up, and it was a thrill to visit his home. I found to my surprise that he was a friend of Harry Leon Wilson, and had probably read *Bunker Bean* himself.

The most exciting thing I learned from my first visit to Jack London's home was that he had a need to produce words to maintain his lifestyle. For many years, he was the highest earning author in the United States, regularly earning $75,000 a year, which is the equivalent of a million dollars a year in today's terms. To earn this amount of money, he had to keep on producing, and he did this by writing one thousand words every day. He did this for twenty years, without missing a day.

I vividly remember the excitement that surged through me when I read that Jack London wrote a thousand words a day. If I wrote a thousand words a day, every day, surely I'd eventually write enough saleable words to become a full-time writer.

A strange thing happened when I returned home. I mistakenly remembered that Jack London had written two thousand words a day. Consequently, when I began modeling his work habits, I wrote two thousand words every day. It was easier than I expected. Once I got into the habit of doing it, I found I could produce the required number of words every day. I was shocked when I returned to Jack London's house fifteen years later and found that I had written twice the number of words that I needed to do to effectively model my work habits on him.

I experienced another benefit from visiting Jack London's home. I had come to the conclusion that writing was too difficult a business. It was too hard to break in, and then, even once you were in, it was too hard to make a living at it. I had spent twenty years of my life scribbling away in my spare time, making some money, but nowhere near enough to justify the number of hours that I had put into it.

However, the desire to be a writer had never left me. Standing in Jack London's living room, I thought about Bunker Bean and writing a thousand words a day, and resolved to become a full-time writer.

Jack London had many more hurdles to overcome than I did. He grew up in poverty, left school at the age of fourteen, and began working at a number of back-breaking menial jobs. At the age of seventeen he spent nine months as a sailor on a sealing expedition. The article he wrote about this experience won a writing competition. The twenty-five dollar prize helped pay the rent on his parents' home.

Jack London then spent five months as a bum, riding the freight trains across the United States. He was arrested and spent a month in jail. He returned home, determined to complete his education, because he was convinced that was the only way he could ever get ahead. He returned to school, a nineteen-year-old in a class of fifteen-year-olds.

After two years at school, he went to a cramming school to try to get into a university. Five weeks into the course he punched his teacher in the nose and, by mutual agreement, left. Undeterred, he studied for nineteen hours a day, and passed the entry exams with distinction. Jack London went to the university, taking all the English courses with the aim of becoming a writer. He left after two semesters.

Jack London then settled down to become a writer. He churned out material, every bit of which was rejected. He received six hundred and fifty rejection slips before he had a single acceptance. Six hundred and fifty! Would you persevere that long? I wouldn't, but I'm not Jack London.

His brother-in-law announced that he was going to Alaska to find gold in the Klondike. Jack London went with him. They were away almost two years, and at the end of it Jack London had $4.50 worth of gold. However, on the way home, he decided that he could write about Alaska, and make money out of his experiences. It worked. At the age of twenty-four, he became a published author. Three years later, *Call of the Wild* was published and at the age of twenty-seven he was America's best-known writer. Jack London's novel, *Martin Eden,* is largely about his own struggles to become a writer.

I considered him a good role model, because of his persistence and also because of his habit of disciplining himself to produce a certain number of words every day. There were other aspects of his character that I did not like. He was racist, for instance, and believed that the world was created purely for the benefit of white Anglo-Saxons. However, he was a product of his times and was not the only person who thought that way at the start of the twentieth century.

| ERLE STANLEY GARDNER

Jack London was the first person on whom I consciously modeled myself. Erle Stanley Gardner was the second. Gardner was a lawyer who hated being a lawyer. As it had taken him five years to become a lawyer, he decided to allow himself five years to become a writer. He intended to give up law if he could make as much money from writing as he did as a lawyer. As he was a partner in a successful law firm, making $12,000 a year (he began writing seriously in 1921), it seemed unlikely that he could achieve this goal. Here is how he fared:

Year One: $974.00

Year Two: $3,436.00

Year Three: $5,838.15

Year Four: $6,627.50

Year Five: $9,614.25

This did not meet his goal, but Gardner had become addicted to writing. In a letter he wrote to encourage prospective writers, Gardner wrote: "Finally, I became so fascinated with writing that I couldn't quit it now to save me. If the editors quit accepting my stories, or quit paying for them, I'd keep on writing just the same."[1]

Gardner made the right decision to give up law. In the following year he earned $13,612.50 and the year after brought in $14,941.00.

Like Jack London, he knew nothing about the business. After a busy day as a lawyer, he would sit down and churn out short stories for the pulp magazines. When he began, his rejection rate was 90 percent. This was largely because he never revised anything. His first draft was his final copy. The pulp magazines paid him between one and three cents a word, so it wasn't worth spending too much time on revision. Incidentally, this also explains why Erle Stanley Gardner's heroes, despite being crack shots, could never kill the villain with less than six bullets. Every time he wrote "bang," he earned at least one cent.

Even after Gardner became one of the most successful writers in the world, he still wanted to know how he could improve. He regularly asked editors for advice. No matter how successful we become, we can still learn. This is one of the most valuable things I learned from Erle Stanley Gardner. I regularly ask for advice and have profited greatly from it.

Two well-known authors who have profited greatly from asking questions are Jack Canfield and Mark Victor Hansen, creators of the *Chicken Soup* books. They asked top-selling authors, such as M. Scott

Peck, Wayne Dyer, Harvey McKay, Barbara De Angelis, and Betty Eadie, what they should do to market and promote their books. They listened carefully, followed their advice—and today Canfield and Hansen are multimillionaires.

Just recently I spoke to an author who was extremely upset with the suggestions his copy editor had made about his latest book. Instead of appreciating the suggestions, thinking about them, and perhaps taking heed of some of them, he ignored them totally. He lost a valuable opportunity to learn. The copy editor was making suggestions that he or she thought would improve the book. Despite this author's feelings, the copy editor was on his side. He was making the common error of thinking the copy editor's suggestions were a personal attack on his precious words. I am grateful to my copy editors for their input, and always take their advice seriously. I am willing to do anything that will make my books better. The better my books are, the more likely they are to sell.

Interestingly, Gardner also had a mentor on whom he modeled himself, a man named William Wallace Cook. Like Gardner, Cook was stuck in a job he hated, and became a writer to enjoy the freedom that this career offered. When he died in 1933, he was described as "the man who deforested Canada" because of the huge amount of paper that had been used to print his works. Cook wrote a couple of books that influenced Gardner profoundly. They were *The Fiction Factory*, which described how he had become successful as a writer, and *Plotto*, which was advertised as "a new method of plot suggestion for writers of creative fiction." William Wallace Cook considered his books to be a product. He wrote:

"A writer is neither better nor worse than any man who happens to be in trade. He is a manufacturer. . . . If the product is good it passes at face value and becomes a medium of exchange."[2]

This is good advice for anyone who wants to establish a long-term career as a writer. You are in business, the writing business. Freeman Lewis, Gardner's paperback publisher, believed he knew Gardner's secret of success: "It often seemed to me that he operated as a professional in an area inhabited largely by amateurs."

Gardner believed in writing everything down. As a result of this, the Gardner collection at the University of Texas contains millions of items. Gardner believed that you should plan first, and then work the plan.

This was some of the best advice I ever received. Like many would-be writers, I daydreamed about the great books I was going to write. I thought up interesting characters, intriguing plots, and incredible surprise endings—but they were all in my head. Once I started writing my thoughts down, my career moved ahead rapidly.

The final piece of advice that I learned from Erle Stanley Gardner (which he had earlier learned from William Wallace Cook) was to keep up-to-date with technology. My first book was written on an old manual typewriter. I kept using it until it finally wore out. I then bought a word processor, and eventually a computer. I was forced into buying them at the time. These days I replace my equipment regularly.

Gardner wrote more than a million words a year. In fact, he was so prolific that rumors spread suggesting that he employed ghost writers. His publisher offered a $100,000 reward to anyone who could prove that Gardner did not write all his own work.

William Wallace Cook always used the latest technology, and Erle Stanley Gardner did the same. He was one of the first authors to have a word counter on his typewriter, and was the first author to use an electric typewriter (in 1925). He believed strongly in anything that could speed up production or make his job easier. Imagine how many words he'd be producing today with the technology that is available now.

An interesting fact about Jack London and Erle Stanley Gardner is that they both left school after punching a teacher in the face. Obviously, I am not suggesting that you copy every aspect of the people you choose to model.

When I suggest that you model yourself on an author you admire, I'm suggesting that you copy their methods of work. This is what Erle Stanley Gardner did when he modeled himself on William Wallace Cook. I am not suggesting that you copy anyone else's style. It is impossible to do this successfully. Back in the eighteenth century Georges LeClerk de Buffon said: "Style is the man himself." Why settle for being a second-rate someone else, when you can be a magnificent, one-of-a-kind you?

You will have noticed that neither Jack London nor Erle Stanley Gardner could be considered New Age authors.[3] Jack London did use New Age themes in some of his plots, but did not believe in them. There are a number of New Age authors who I admire greatly, but unfortunately, I do not know enough about their methods of work to use them as models. It does not matter what type of writing the people you choose to model are engaged in. The important thing is to read about them and learn how they achieved their goals of becoming successful writers. Obviously, the people you choose must have had a strong belief that they had something to offer as writers, and were prepared to work hard to achieve their goals. Study successful authors and adopt some of their work habits.

... No matter how successful we become, we can still learn from other writers ...

| WHAT I LEARNED FROM JACK LONDON

Know What You Want—Jack London wanted to be a writer and was prepared to do whatever was necessary to achieve that goal.

Persistence—Jack London received more than 650 rejections before selling anything.

Push Yourself—Jack London set himself a daily limit of 1,000 words, and did this for more than twenty years.

Promotion—Jack London was one of the first authors to actively promote himself and his books. As a result, he became the biggest-selling author in the United States.

Take Time Off—Jack London did not do this, and died before his fortieth birthday.

WHAT I LEARNED FROM ERLE STANLEY GARDNER

Set a Time Limit—He gave himself five years to make more money from writing than he did from being a lawyer.

Ask Questions—You can always improve. Follow Erle Stanley Gardner's advice and ask questions, even after you've become successful.

You Are Selling a Product—You are in business, and words are your product.

Plan First, Then Work the Plan—Get it down on paper.

Keep Up-to-date with Technology—Buy the best equipment you can afford, and upgrade regularly. Anything that saves you time and effort is a good investment.

Study the Market—When Erle Stanley Gardner decided to write mystery novels in the 1930s he became a life-long student of the genre. He analyzed the structure, construction, and form of everything he read, constantly trying to find out why some things worked while others did not.

Reply to Letters—At one time, Gardner was writing 20,000 words of correspondence a day.[4] He wrote to his publisher telling him that during a ten-year period he "averaged 462.5 pages of single-spaced correspondence for every 225.7 double-spaced pages of book ms [manuscript]."

| The Master Mind Group

In his hugely successful book, *Think and Grow Rich*, Napoleon Hill devoted an entire chapter to the concept of a Master Mind group. This is a group of two or more people who meet regularly with the purpose of achieving a specific aim. I belong to two Master Mind groups and have benefited enormously from my involvement with them.

The first Master Mind group I belong to has five members, and we meet once a month for breakfast. I was a little bit dubious about joining this group, as my goals are different to the other members, who are all professional speakers. Although I do a lot of speaking, I see myself primarily as a writer. Their goals, not surprisingly, relate to advancing in their speaking careers. To my surprise, the fact that we have different goals has been helpful. We are able to help each other with our different points of view. In this group we discuss virtually anything, and our goals relate to every area of our lives. The progress of every member of this group over the last three years has been incredible.

My writing Master Mind group consists of four people. We are all published authors. One has written a series of successful business management books and is trying to establish a series of popular action novels. The second has written a series of humorous books, and is now working on more serious topics. The third is working on novels of suspense, and is currently ghost writing as well. I write mainly for the New Age market. We meet once a month for lunch.

We are not a writer's group in the normal sense of the word. We do not read to each other what we have produced. In fact, we seldom discuss what we are working on. Instead, we talk about the pleasures and difficulties of being full-time writers. We discuss various ways of marketing and promoting our wares. We share our successes and disappointments.

One of the greatest benefits for me is the regular interaction with other people who are in the same business. Writing can be lonely, and it is good to be able to talk openly about any facet of the writing field with friends who are also writers. Although we meet officially once a month, we see each other more frequently than that for informal lunches, dinners, or drinks. We also communicate by phone and e-mail.

One of us has been knocked back a few times with his most recent novel. No matter how experienced you are, rejection is a fact of life for all writers. It has been helpful for him to express his feelings to the rest of us, and we have made suggestions as to what he should do next. As a result, he has found himself another agent and is hard at work on his next book.

... writing can be lonely—it is good to talk with friends who are also writers ...

Likewise, we celebrate our successes. One of our members sold nine books to a single publisher. Three of these were written, and the others were outlined. We were all thrilled for him, as we knew how much time and effort he had put into them. Earlier this year, I signed two book contracts in a single week, one for a nonfiction book and the other for a novel. I was thrilled with this, and so were the other members of my Master Mind group.

We are a social, fun-loving group, and we have all benefited from our association.

You will find it helpful to surround yourself with a few people who are also aspiring authors. Take your time and choose carefully. You do not want bitter, backstabbing, negative people who are jealous of your success. I used to belong to a magic club and know far too much about that sort of person. It is important that the members of your Master Mind group are positive, open, and honest. If you choose your associates wisely, you will find that your writing career will take a quantum leap forward.

Today, it is possible to have a Master Mind group over the Internet. I belong to a group of New Age authors who regularly post messages to each other on a private newsgroup. There are twenty of us, so it is an association of similar-minded New Age authors, rather than a Master Mind group. However, if you know a few like-minded people around the world, you could easily set up a Master Mind group on the Internet.

You will probably also be tempted to join different writing groups and associations. Think carefully before joining any of them. These groups provide a valuable service to their members, but their goals are likely to be different from yours. Their members are likely to be enthusiastic amateurs who like the idea of writing more than the writing itself. You will meet pleasant people at these groups, but they will do nothing to help your writing career. I belong to an association of authors who see themselves as "literary," and do not wholly approve of people who make money from their writing. One of the members told me that he wants to be famous after he is dead. I enjoy their meetings because of the interesting people who belong, but it has done nothing to help my writing career.

3

LEARNING TO WRITE

To be successful in the New Age market, you not only have to be knowledgeable about your subject, and have the necessary determination to work at your book until it is finished. You also need to write in such a way that your readers can understand what you are telling them.

Is it possible to learn how to write? The answer is both yes and no. Although it is not possible to teach someone how to write great literary works, it is possible to teach anyone who is able to talk lucidly how to communicate effectively with words on paper. The craft of writing can be taught. The art of writing cannot.

There are night school courses that teach writing. There are also mail-order courses, books, and writers' conferences and seminars. These can all be helpful, but you need to choose them with care. The person teaching creative writing at your local high school may not have published anything, but might be a superb teacher. In this case, he or she would make a better instructor than an author who has published a dozen books, but finds it hard to speak in public. Learn as much as you can about the course and the teachers before you start.

| DEVELOPING AN ENGAGING STYLE

When writing for publication it is vital that your writing be clear, accurate, easy to understand, and enjoyable to read. Some nonfiction books read like novels because the author has a pleasant, engaging style that carries the reader effortlessly along. Books of this sort will always be more popular than similar works that are hard to read. One of your aims must be to write the most readable book that you can. I consider myself part of the entertainment industry. If someone has to choose between going to the movies or buying my book, I want him or her to buy my book.

| ORGANIZING YOUR THOUGHTS

People must also understand, and be able to use, the information that you have given them. Robert Louis Stevenson certainly understood this. He wrote: "Don't write merely to be understood. Write so you cannot possibly be misunderstood."[1]

Arranging your thoughts in a logical sequence helps your readers to understand. Start with a general statement that your reader already knows, and then add additional facts, one at a time, until you have made your point.

| USEFUL TOOLS

Naturally, you will need a variety of tools to help you. The most important of these is a good dictionary. I use *The Random House Dictionary of the English Language*. Whenever you are not sure of the exact meaning of a word, look it up before using it. Mark Twain wrote: "The difference between the right word and the almost right word is the difference between lightning and a lightning bug." You must use the right words to be understood.

You should also look up words whenever you are unsure of the spelling. Your word processing program will probably have a spell-check facility, but you will learn more by looking up any doubtful words in a dictionary and reading the definition when you check for the correct spelling.

You will also need Strunk and White's classic book, *The Elements of Style*. If you study this small book carefully, you will learn everything you need to know about writing. *The Chicago Manual of Style*, published by the University of Chicago Press, is another book that should also be in your library. It is the standard manual used by most publishers.

You will find a good thesaurus useful, also. However, use it only to find the perfect word to express yourself. Most of the time, the simplest word is the best. Make sure that you are aware of the subtle nuances in meaning before choosing a word from a thesaurus. When I looked up "occult" in my thesaurus, I found: esoteric, mystic, mysterious, anagogic, metapsychic, metaphysic, cabalic, cabalistic, supernatural, and theosophic. To my mind, most of these words would not clarify or define "occult" to someone who was not familiar with the term.

| COMMON ERRORS

You will need at least a basic understanding of English grammar. Grammar is the word used to describe the science and structure of language. Some writers use grammar instinctively, and would be hard put to explain the difference between an adjective and an adverb. In fact, they may not even know what an adverb is. However, these authors know how to arrange their words in the best possible order and, consequently, do not need to know the correct terminology. However, many beginning writers need help in this regard.

Recently, I was one of the judges for a national novel writing competition, and was astounded at the number of entrants who were incapable of writing a sentence. A sentence is a group of words that expresses a complete thought. It usually contains both a subject and predicate (a statement made about the subject). An example would be

"Tom fired the gun." However, a sentence can sometimes consist of just one word. "Fire!" is a complete sentence. Words are the basic building blocks that we use to express ourselves. If you are going to write for publication you must know how to arrange these words into sentences, paragraphs, chapters, and books.

The other main problem with the entries to the novel writing competition was that few of the entrants got straight to the point. Instead of starting with an exciting scene, most began with a leisurely account of the incidents leading up to the action. Getting to the point is just as important in nonfiction.

... the craft of writing can be taught—the art of writing can not ...

You attended classes in grammar when you were at school. Consequently, at least at one time, you knew the differences between nouns and verbs and adjectives. If you feel the need to brush up on your skills in these areas, see what classes are available near your home. A brief refresher course will hone your skills and make your writing more saleable. A course in creative writing will also prove useful if you have written nothing for a long while.

You do not need to spend years at college gaining a degree in writing. Many famous writers had little in the way of formal education. William Faulkner and Ernest Hemingway, for instance, did not go to college. The best education is to write as much as you can. The more writing you do, the better you will become.

At the very least, you will need to know how verbs, nouns, adjectives, and adverbs work. These are the most important parts of speech. (The others are conjunctions, interjections, prepositions, and pronouns.)

Verbs are used to express action (the bird *flew*) or a state of being (she *is tired*). They are the only parts of speech that express voice (I, you, he, she, it, we, they). Verbs can be active or passive. An active verb is more powerful than a passive one. "Bill *fired* the gun" (active), is stronger than "the gun *was fired* by Bill" (passive). For the most part, you should use active verbs because they give strength, vitality, and power to your writing. Passive verbs slow down the pace. They lack energy. However, passive verbs are necessary for variety, and should be used sparingly.

Nouns are naming words. They name people, places, things, ideas, and actions. Man, woman, house, car, and cat are all examples of nouns. Most of the time, the simplest noun is the best as you want your writing to be clear and exact. Consequently, you would normally choose "car" over "motorized vehicle."

A pronoun is a word used instead of a noun. "Him" is an example of a pronoun in the following sentence: "She saw her boyfriend on the other side of the road, but did not call out to *him*." Naturally, it must be clear who you are referring to. Look at this example: "Dr. Rhine and Hubert Pearce sat opposite each other at the table. His task was to guess which card would appear next." This is confusing, as the "his" could mean either Dr. Rhine or Hubert Pearce.

Adjectives are describing words that change, modify, or qualify the meaning of nouns. They usually come immediately before or after the noun they are qualifying. Many beginning writers overuse adjectives. "He sat on the fence" is a perfectly good sentence. However, when we add an adjective and write: "He sat on the weather-beaten fence," we provide more information. Too many adjectives weaken rather than strengthen the overall picture. Use adjectives to strengthen nouns only when necessary. The quality of your writing will improve as a result.

Adverbs are used to modify verbs and adjectives. They are easy to detect, as they usually end with -ly (she dealt the cards casually). Like adjectives, they should be used with caution.

Your writing will usually be better, and more effective, when you limit the use of adverbs and adjectives. It is impossible to write without them, but use nouns and verbs as much as possible.

Your writing should contain a mixture of short and long sentences. Short sentences are easy to follow and understand, but too many of them make the writing appear jerky. If you create too many long sentences your writing will seem heavy, pedantic, and boring. Writers of textbooks are frequently guilty of this. Varying the lengths of your sentences makes for stimulating writing.

Your sentence structure should vary, also. The writing appears dull when a series of sentences follow the standard subject-verb-object formula. This is particularly the case when you are explaining something that happened to you.

Authors sometimes get into the habit of starting many sentences in the same way. "It is" is a common example. Starting almost every sentence with "I" can be just as irritating, and make the author appear egotistical. Here is an example: "I picked up the pendulum and suspended it over the map. I thought of the missing cat's name as I slowly moved the pendulum across the map. I felt a slight movement when the pendulum was over the right-hand corner. I paused and stopped the movement of the pendulum with my free hand. I took a deep breath, and held the pendulum over the spot where it had moved. I was certain that it was telling me that the cat was in that area." The above quotation is providing the necessary information, but is tedious to read. Here is another version of the same incident: "I suspended the pendulum over the map. 'Tibbles,' I murmured. 'Where are you, Tibbles?' As I slowly moved the pendulum across the map, it made a slight movement over the right-hand corner. Could the missing cat have gone this far? I stopped the movement of the pendulum, and held it over the spot where it had moved before. Again, the pendulum responded positively." In the second version, only two sentences start with "I," and the total number is reduced from seven to four. I hope you agree that this version is more pleasant to read than the first one.

As a general rule, the average number of words in your sentences should be less than twenty. Your readers will not realize why they are enjoying reading your words, but will be carried along with the variety of sentence types.

Your paragraphs should also vary in length. Long paragraphs can intimidate your readers. If someone is browsing through your book in a bookstore and finds page after page of dense prose, he or she is likely to replace it, and search for a book that contains more white space. This may not be done consciously, but at a subliminal level your potential reader is looking for something that is both informative and readable.

I know that there are exceptions. William Faulkner's paragraphs were sometimes two or three pages long. Of course, he was a genius who was exploring the limits of his form. Also, he was writing fiction, rather than nonfiction. If you are a genius, you might get away with paragraphs that go on and on. I want my readers to enjoy my books, and am not prepared to take that sort of risk. With nonfiction, you are always trying to explain things as clearly and as succinctly as possible.

... clichés may be acceptable in speech, but not in print ...

Do you know people who talk endlessly, but say little? Many books are like that. Be specific and concise. Choose your words carefully and be as brief as possible. Naturally, everything has to be explained fully, but use no more words than are necessary.

Use short words in preference to long words. Some writers think that by using long words they will impress their readers with their knowledge and erudition. Instead of achieving this, they usually write prose that is difficult to read. Everything you write should be written with the aim of helping your readers to understand and learn as much as possible. Anything that interferes with this should be eliminated. Consequently, as well as using short words, use simple, rather than complex, words.

"Avoid clichés like the plague" has become a popular one-liner, and is advice all writers should follow. Clichés that might be acceptable in daily conversation make the author appear lazy when used in a book. It is better to either come up with something fresh, or to perhaps change the cliché in some way to give it a new twist.

Whenever possible, use gender-neutral terms. You might use chair, or chairperson, instead of chairman, for example. A fireman would become a firefighter, an airline steward would become a flight attendant, and a mailman a mail carrier. This is not simply an exercise in political correctness; these terms are more correct.

Pronouns are more difficult. A number of years ago, it was common for writers to use "he" all the way through their books. This was unintentional sexism, and was intended to include both male and female. This is no longer acceptable, but it can create problems for writers. One effective solution is to use a plural, rather than singular, subject. Alternatively, you can use "he or she" and "his and her" if you wish to retain the singular case. "The candidate will be raised to the 49th degree when he passes the examination,"would be considered sexist today. It can be rewritten in the plural: "Candidates will be raised to the 49th degree when they pass the examination," or kept in the singular: "The candidate will be raised to the 49th degree when he or she passes the examination."

All of this may sound too difficult. In fact, the recipe is simple: write the way you would like to be able to talk. Some people are highly articulate and possess good conversational skills. When these people write, they sometimes express themselves in exactly the way they would in everyday conversation. However, most of us are not blessed with these skills. Fortunately, though, we can learn to write in the style in which we would like to be able to speak. Even people who speak fluently often become stilted when they start to write.

Your writing should be conversational and easy to read. Consequently, it is a good habit to read your writing out loud. Pause whenever you reach a comma, semicolon, or period. Any awkward or unnatural phrases will become apparent as soon as you read aloud. Your ear usually catches more than your eye.

Writing has one huge advantage over speaking. You can change anything you like afterward. I am sure that after many conversations, you thought of all the clever remarks you could have said. This problem is not a factor when you are writing. If you think of a better way of expressing something later on, you can go back and change it.

| BENJAMIN FRANKLIN'S METHOD

Benjamin Franklin devised a technique to improve his writing skills. His deceptively simple method enables you to learn the art of writing from any authors you admire. Start by choosing about two thousand words from an author who writes the type of material you want to write. Summarize the material in about two hundred words. Put your summary away for a few days, and then, without looking at the original script, write your own version of the ideas in about two thousand words. Once you have done this, compare your version with the original. This analysis will allow you to see the differences between your writing and that of the published author. Spend time doing this, observing what he or she did that was better than what you wrote. Conversely, you may find things that you wrote that you consider better than the published author's effort. Once you have done this, put your summary away again for another few days, and then repeat the exercise. Do this with as many published authors as you can.

| LOVE YOUR SUBJECT

The best advice I can give is to write about topics that you love. If you write about subjects that captivate and inspire you, your enthusiasm will be picked up by your readers. You will never lack readers if you write about subjects that you are bursting to tell others.

| WRITE REGULARLY

Everything described in this chapter will become automatic over time. The important thing is to write regularly, every day if possible. Some people find keeping a journal an excellent way of recording their thoughts, and this can be a useful way of disciplining yourself to write regularly. Letter writing is another method. Fortunately, there is a third method that will enable you to practice while writing for the New Age market.

There are many New Age newspapers and magazines that are always looking for articles. Although most of these do not pay for submissions, they provide good opportunities for practice. Every now and again, an editor at one of these newspapers will offer advice. Any feedback is good. He or she is trying to help you improve.

The other advantage of writing free articles is that you will gradually build up a "clip file" of articles you have written. These show prospective publishers that you are disciplined, able to write, and are interested in making a career as a New Age writer.

Ambition is the most important quality for a would-be writer. I met many talented writers while teaching my *Wake Up and Write!* seminars. However, I have not heard of any of them since. This is because they lacked the necessary persistence, determination, and ambition to become successful. This is the most important quality of all. Someone with average writing ability but huge determination will invariably become more successful than a talented writer who gives up easily.

4
Choosing the Right Publisher

Most beginning authors write a book and then think about finding a publisher. This is the hard way to do it, as you may have to send your manuscript to dozens of publishers before it finds a home. This is a huge waste of time, postage, and nervous energy, especially as the chances of it being accepted are remote.

Although it may sound strange, it makes much more sense to choose the publisher before you write a single word. Publishers need authors. Despite the gloomy stories you are bound to hear from unpublished authors, publishers are always looking for authors who can write the sort of books that they want to publish. All you have to do is give them exactly what they want.

| The First Step

The first step is to find out who the potential publishers are for the type of book that you want to write. *Writer's Market* and *Literary Marketplace* are two excellent resources that list publishers by the types of works they are interested in. These books are updated every year. Older editions of these books are fine, if you are simply checking out a category of publisher. However, you need the most up-to-date edition for specific information. Publishing houses are businesses, and sometimes they get taken over, or go out of business. Sometimes the nature of the business can change, too. Checking the publishers out in these books also tells you some of their requirements. Here is where you will learn if they accept unagented manuscripts, for instance.

As well as looking for potential publishers in these books, spend time in bookstores and libraries to see who has published books that are similar to the one you are planning to write.

Make a list of all the publishers who you think would be suitable, and contact them requesting their author guidelines.

| SUBMISSION GUIDELINES

Fortunately, most publishers are happy to provide prospective authors with submission guidelines. In fact, I would advise you to avoid publishers who do not have guidelines. They obviously have little regard for their authors, and cannot be bothered telling you what they are looking for. Llewellyn has three sets of guidelines: one each for books, artwork, and Tarot and divination decks.

The guidelines are enormously helpful to authors, as they tell them what the publisher is looking for. They are also useful to the publishers, as they enable them to explain as much as possible ahead of time. The guidelines save a great deal of time and expense in corresponding with inexperienced authors who are not familiar with the publishing process.

Most publishers' guidelines can be downloaded from their websites, or by sending them a stamped, self-addressed envelope. A careful study of these will tell you exactly what the publisher is looking for.

Yet, despite this, every publisher receives huge numbers of manuscripts from people who have not bothered to read the guidelines. Naturally, virtually all of these manuscripts get returned. Nowadays, of course, many publishers do not return rejected manuscripts, but send a form rejection letter instead.

I even know someone who sent a manuscript to a publisher after reading in the guidelines that they had no interest in the subject she had written on. She told me that her book was so good that the publisher would accept it anyway. Needless to say, after wasting her own time, and that of the staff in the publisher's office, her manuscript came back.

This sort of thing should never happen. Professional authors do their homework and study the market before writing their books.

Llewellyn Worldwide, Ltd., my publisher, has a "Submission Guidelines Information Package." The first page tells you what their subject areas are, and explains that they are looking for practical, how-to-do-it books. It also tells prospective authors that they "do not publish 'about' books, collections of poetry, or biographies." If you send them a collection of New Age verse, it will come straight back.

The second page tells you how to submit a manuscript to them. The specifications and correct formatting of the manuscript are also covered here. Like most publishers today, Llewellyn requires a copy of the manuscript on disk, as well as a printed-out, or "hard" copy. On this page you also learn that Llewellyn will look at both completed manuscripts and book proposals. A book proposal is an outline of the proposed book, and two or three sample chapters. Llewellyn also looks at multiple submissions. This is when you send your manuscript to a number of different publishers at the same time.

Page three describes additional material that Llewellyn readers find useful: a table of contents, an index, a glossary, and a bibliography. This material also helps sell your book into libraries. Not all of these are essential for every book, but should be included if they can help your prospective reader.

The guidelines continue by explaining the editing process, and how Llewellyn aims to produce a book that pleases both the publisher and author.

A section covers how to gain permission to use quotations from other published sources. At the back of the guidelines is a form that can be used when seeking permission from copyright holders.

As well as requiring permission for use of other people's material, Llewellyn also needs proper attribution and documentation of any outside sources. These are usually included in the bibliography.

Llewellyn prefers that you do not hire an illustrator, and include a page of information on artwork and photographs.

The next section of the guidelines explains how Llewellyn will promote and market your book. Your book will be promoted in Llewellyn's trade catalogs, and possibly in *New Worlds* magazine. When possible, Llewellyn's publicity and promotion department will work with you to arrange author interviews and marketing events. Llewellyn distributes their books internationally, and actively seeks foreign market sales for their books. They also sell the rights for foreign language editions of their books.

At the end of the guidelines is an author questionnaire. This tells Llewellyn about you, your background, and expertise. It also provides them with the information they need to effectively publicize and promote you and your book. The answers to the questions in this section often appear as part of the front matter for your book.

Llewellyn's guidelines are more comprehensive than most I have seen. I have seen authors gasp when they read the amount of information they need to provide, in addition to the manuscript. However, it is all done for a purpose. If you follow the guidelines to the letter, and write an outstanding book that relates to one of Llewellyn's areas of interest (complete with permissions and citation), and then send it to them in the correct format, with a comprehensively answered author's questionnaire, your book will be published.

On the other hand, if you ignore the guidelines and send in a handwritten manuscript, or something that does not relate to their areas of interest, you will deservedly receive your manuscript back.

Naturally, you should study the guidelines carefully before writing your book. You should consult them from time to time while writing it, and then study them again before submitting your manuscript. Make sure that your manuscript is set out and submitted in exactly the form the publisher wants. If the guidelines specify that the manuscript is double-spaced, your manuscript needs to be double-spaced. If the publisher also requires the text on disk, as Llewellyn does, make sure to include it, in the format specified in the guidelines. Finally, ensure that your manuscript is neat, as neatness always counts.

You can relate your manuscript and author's questionnaire to a job interview. Naturally, you dress well and try to make a good impression when you are being interviewed for a position. You show interest and enthusiasm, as you are selling yourself. You will have done your homework and checked out the company and its products. Consequently, you will be able to ask relevant and intelligent questions. Your potential employer will want to know all about you. The publisher to whom you send your manuscript will also want to know as much as possible about you. They will learn this from your manuscript and your answers to the author's questionnaire. This package is designed to sell you to the publisher. Consequently, you cannot spend too much time making your "sales" package as presentable as possible.

| GIVE YOUR PUBLISHERS WHAT THEY WANT

As I said at the start of this chapter, all you need to do is give the publisher what he or she wants. It is as simple, and as hard, as that.

In addition to studying the guidelines you should also read a selection of your proposed publisher's books. Before submitting my first book to Llewellyn I bought a dozen of their most recent books to study. I deliberately chose books that I would not have bought normally, as I wanted to gain a feel for the types of books they published. I found this extremely useful, and recommend that you do the same.

By doing this you will gain insights that go far beyond the guidelines. Study the books individually and as a group. This will help you learn your prospective publisher's way of doing things. Every publisher has a house style that can only be determined by studying books that he or she has published.

Take your time doing all of this. This is valuable research that will enable you to write the book that your prospective publisher is dying to publish.

In the next chapter we will finally start work on outlining the book that your publisher is waiting for.

5

How to Outline Your Book

You are finally ready to start work on your book. You have chosen a topic, found a need for it, decided on a publisher, and written a synopsis.

This is all some authors need. They do not need a comprehensive outline of their proposed book to get started. I would find it difficult to write this way, but any method that works for you is the best method to use. I know several authors who consider outlines to be a waste of time. They feel that it restricts them and hampers their creativity. These people consistently write successful books without outlining them first.

I look at outlines differently. An outline is like a road map that tells me everything I want to include in the book. It shows me where I'm going. If I know where I'm going and have a road map to guide me, the chances are that I will ultimately reach my destination. A builder would never build a house without a set of plans. My outline represents my plan for the book. However, unlike the builder's plans, my outline is never complete. I constantly add to it and make changes while writing the book. This gives me the freedom to be as spontaneous as people who do not use outlines. However, when I make a change, I can then make whatever adjustments are needed to my outline to ensure that the book still finishes in the right place. Consequently, my outline is never complete.

The major argument against using an outline is that the book invariably changes while you are writing it. This is especially true if you are researching while you are writing. However, it is a simple matter to change the outline when necessary, and I feel that the advantages far outweigh any disadvantages.

One advantage of using an outline is that you are much more likely to finish the book. I have several unfinished books hidden away in a drawer. I did not use an outline with any of them. When problems occurred with the project, it seemed easier to abandon the exercise rather than continue struggling with it. That problem has never arisen with an outlined book. If I get temporarily stuck somewhere, I can simply move to another chapter and work on that. When I return to the section that was causing difficulty, the problem will usually have disappeared. I have finished every book I started since forcing myself to use an outline.

With an outline I always know what to write next. The outline enables me to organize my thoughts before I start writing. This means that I never suffer from writer's block because I always know what comes next.

An outline also makes the writing of the book less daunting. Writing a book of sixty or eighty thousand words may seem like an impossible task, but once the book is outlined, you can focus on writing just one chapter, followed by another, until the book is finished.

I can also write the chapters in any order I choose. If my outline tells me that something is explained in chapter three, for instance, I can write chapter eleven before starting chapter three without explaining whatever it happens to be again. This saves me time and effort when it comes time to revise the book. I hate having to delete words that should not have been written in the first place.

An outline also ensures that the final manuscript is properly balanced. Your book will be well structured and will progress in a logical way. Writers who simply let their thoughts flow usually have to spend more time editing and revising their books than people who work to a plan.

The outline ensures that I cover every aspect of the subject. When I plan to write a book on a certain topic, I will already know a reasonable amount about it. However, there will be areas where my knowledge is limited, or even nonexistent. The outline reminds me of these, and ensures that I do enough research on the missing areas to be able to offer my readers a complete coverage of the subject.

Finally, an outline lets me write the book more quickly and effectively. As I already know what information is required for each chapter, all I have to do is write it. There is no need to spend additional time looking for, or thinking about, whatever material is required.

One additional benefit of creating an outline is that, by the time I have completed it, I will know approximately how long the book will be. If each chapter contains roughly three thousand words, and I have outlined twenty chapters, I know that the finished book will contain around sixty thousand words. This information can be important. If you are writing a book that is to be part of a series, you do not want to produce a manuscript that is too short or too long compared to the other books in the series.

It is not hard to reduce the size of a manuscript, but it is usually difficult to increase the length of a manuscript without it becoming obvious to the reader. I have found the best way to increase the length of a book is to write additional chapters, rather than trying to increase the length of the existing chapters with padding. Naturally, it is better to write a book of the required length in the first place.

As you can see, I firmly believe in outlines. If you are about to write your first book, I would say that an outline is essential. If you are about to write your thirtieth book, I would still recommend that you create an outline first.

| HOW TO CREATE AN OUTLINE

There are many ways of creating outlines. I usually start with a stack of blank file cards. I write each chapter heading on a different card and then look at them one at a time. I think about what needs to be covered in that particular chapter, and record this information on the file card. I then ask myself what else could be included in that chapter. Any ideas that present themselves are written on the card.

At this stage, I don't evaluate any of the ideas. I write down everything that occurs to me, no matter how ludicrous it may appear. By the time this exercise is finished, I have a stack of file cards, each representing one chapter in the book. Some of these file cards will be covered with ideas, while others will have only a few notes written on them.

I usually carry these file cards around with me for a day or two, adding ideas as they occur to me. I carry a few extra cards, also, in case they are needed. I might get an idea for an extra chapter, or possibly have so many ideas for one chapter that I need more than one card to record them all.

At the end of this process I examine the cards again, and write the questions that I would like to see answered in each chapter. These are standard who, what, where, when, why, and how questions. I like to have several questions for each chapter. If I come up with only a few questions, it is a sign that I probably do not have enough material for a complete chapter. In this case, I will consider eliminating that chapter, or combining it with another. The opposite also applies. If I come up with too many questions I may decide to split the chapter into two or three.

I may decide to change the order in which the chapters appear. Having my chapters on file cards means that I can rearrange them as many times as I wish.

I can also examine the cards to make sure that the book is properly balanced. For instance, I might find that I have split up a chapter into three sections. One topic needs twenty pages to cover properly, but the other two can be covered in just a few pages. I can eliminate potential problems of this sort at the outlining stage, and that can save me a great deal of time when it comes to editing the book.

There is no need to hurry over the outlining. Each chapter should cover at least one major aspect of the subject, and it is better to consider this before writing the book, rather than spend time trying to reorganize the book afterward.

| Mind-Mapping and Onions

I now transfer this information onto eight-and-a-half by eleven-inch paper, allowing one page for each chapter. How you do this is entirely up to you. My approach varies from book to book, and even from chapter to chapter. Sometimes I simply write the main points down, allowing plenty of space between them to add any thoughts that occur to me later. This is the method I use if I intend sending the outline to an agent or publisher. In this case the outline consists of the chapter headings, followed by a paragraph explaining what is to be included in each chapter. By doing this, an average book can be described in two or three pages.

Most of the time I use a mind-mapping technique. The chapter heading is written in the center of the paper and is surrounded with the other information using a system of lines and arrows to connect all the main points.

A friend of mine calls this the onion technique. The chapter heading in the middle of the page is the inside of the onion. I gradually add layers of information around this center until the onion is complete. Whenever I see this friend, he asks me if I have all my onions.

Usually, I outline the entire book in this way before starting to write. However, every now and again, I outline a chapter and then write it, before repeating the process with the next chapter.

Once the book, or chapter, has been outlined, I look at each of the points and list them in the order I want them to appear in the chapter.

Again, this frequently changes while I am writing. I may find that one point flows into the next more easily in a different order to the one I had envisaged. That is not a problem. I simply renumber the remaining points to ensure that nothing gets left out accidentally.

At this stage I also make notes about the anecdotes, stories, case histories, quotations, and anything else that I plan to include in the book. These are all intended to illustrate different points, but they also make the book more enjoyable to read.

I then find it best to put the outline aside for a few days and focus on other things. Naturally, I'll make notes about anything that occurs to me, but I try not to think too much about the book during this time.

After a few days, I go through the outline chapter by chapter. I look at it with a number of aims in mind:

1. I want to make sure that everything that should be included in the book is there. It is surprisingly easy to accidentally omit something.

2. I want to make sure that the material flows in the right order, so that the reader will learn all about the subject in a clear, logical manner.

3. I want to make a separate list of anything that still needs to be researched, so that I can start work on that right away.

Once I feel that the outline is complete and comprehensive enough, I start writing. If the outline seems to be lacking in some way, I'll go back to my file cards and start the process again. Even though I know the outline will change while I am writing the book, it is still important for me to feel that it covers the subject in sufficient detail before I start writing.

I have written a number of books without an outline, but find that the time spent creating an outline enables me to write the book more quickly and more easily. I also think that it results in a better book.

You may remember the quick synopsis I did for a proposed candle magic book:

Introduction—history of candle burning and my own introduction to the subject

What is candle magic?

Types of candles

Color

Fragrance

How to dress a candle

Timing—days of the week, planetary hours

Numerology and candles

Magical alphabets—inscribing candles

Magic squares

Healing with candles

Candle rituals—achieving goals, past lives, contacting angels and guides

That was my original synopsis. By the time I had finished making notes on file cards the outline looked like this:

INTRODUCTION
    History of fire, candles, and candle magick
    My introduction to the subject

Chapter One: WHAT IS CANDLE MAGICK?
    What is magick? Cause and effect
    What is candle magick?
    It can be used to attract, repel, and protect. It can be used for love, money, and health. It can also be used for divination.

Chapter Two: TYPES OF CANDLES
Beeswax candles
Altar candles
Planetary candles
Astral candles
Offertory candles
Novena candles
Other requirements include: spills or tapers, a snuffer, oils,
    censer, incense, altar, candle holders, and a pendulum

Chapter Three: HOW TO MAKE YOUR OWN CANDLES
Beeswax candles
Other types of candles
Ritual involved in making them

Chapter Four: COLOR
Color symbolism
Meanings of the different colors
Positive and negative characteristics of each color
How to select the correct color for different purposes

Chapter Five: FRAGRANCE
Incense
Fragrance and the different planets
Fragrances for each day of the week
Benefits of taking magickal baths

Chapter Six: HOW TO DRESS A CANDLE
Oils
Choosing the correct oil
Cleansing the candle
Oiling the candle
Ritual for charging the candle

Chapter Seven: TIMING
   Using an ephemeris, almanac, or astrological calendar to
      determine the Moon's phases
   Planetary hours
   The Moon in the zodiacal signs
   Days of the week
   Time of birth
   Cosmic vibration from day of birth

Chapter Eight: NUMEROLOGY AND CANDLES
   Life path
   Expression
   Soul urge
   Uses of each for achieving various goals

Chapter Nine: MAGICKAL ALPHABETS
   Inscribing candles
   Alphabets such as Theban, Etruscan, and Templar
   Symbol candles: pentagrams, etc.

Chapter Ten: MAGIC SQUARES
   Magic squares for each day of the week: Sun, Moon, Mars,
      Mercury, Jupiter, Venus, and Saturn
   How to draw these
   Specific colors and purpose for each one
   Ritual for each one

Chapter Eleven: HEALING WITH CANDLES
   Angelic healing
   Other forms of healing
   Healing people
   Healing animals

Chapter Twelve: CANDLE RITUALS
   Achieving goals
   Relieving problems from past lives

Releasing karma

Attracting spirit guides and angel guardians

Achieving happiness, success, prosperity, and love

Chapter Thirteen: CONCLUSION

Deciding what you want and the specific steps for achieving it
using candle magic

If I was not preparing a book proposal to send to a publisher, I would possibly stop at this point, as I now have everything necessary to start writing the book. I am not constrained by these notes. Different things will occur to me as I write, and will be added to my notes.

However, if I was preparing a book proposal to send to an agent or publisher, I would need to flesh out these basic notes, and also provide background information.

| Book Proposals

A book proposal is basically a sales pitch. You are aiming to sell the publisher or agent on the merits of publishing the book that you are planning to write. Consequently, you need to ensure that your writing is positive and irresistible. If the publisher is carried along by your proposal, he or she will envisage you doing the same with your book. A proposal is a package containing a number of elements:

1. A cover letter. This should be addressed to a specific person and be brief and to the point. Mention any previous dealings you may have had with the editor or agent, and say that your proposal for such-and-such a book is enclosed.

2. The proposal needs to include an overview of the book, showing its significance and uniqueness. There is no point in writing a book that is simply a rehash of everything else that is already available. Your book has to contain fresh, new material, and you must point this out in your proposal.

3. Your proposal has to indicate potential marketing possibilities. Who will buy it?

4. Your proposal must refer to other books on the subject, and explain why your book will be better, different, or more complete than anything else that is currently available.

5. Your credentials for writing the book. Why you? Why this particular book?

6. A listing of the chapter titles, with a brief explanation of what will be included in each chapter. It does not matter if you change your mind about some of this while writing the book. The purpose of this is to show your publisher what information you plan to include.

7. One or two sample chapters. This does not have to be the first chapter. Write the chapter, or chapters, that you feel is most likely to appeal to your proposed publisher. The purpose of this is to demonstrate to the publisher that you can write, and are capable of finishing the book.

Here is a sample book proposal based on my file cards. You will notice a number of changes, including a whole new chapter, that occurred to me while I was writing it:

PROPOSAL
Magickal Candles

People have always been fascinated with fire, and it is not surprising that people all around the world have used flame as an accompaniment to prayer and magick for thousands of years. Primitive people danced and sang around fires to invoke the spirits. Today Christianity, Judaism, and Hinduism still associate fire with divinity. Before candles were invented, people used small oil lamps, called votive lamps, when making prayers and offerings to the gods. Beeswax candles were used in Egypt and Crete from about 3000 B.C.E., and helped people to send their prayers to God.

It was a short step from this to using candles for magickal purposes. The rituals of candle magick are simple to perform, but powerful in effect. They utilize role-playing, drama, symbolism, and emotion to achieve their aims. Interestingly, most people first experience candle magick when they are three or four years old. Do you remember blowing out the candles on your birthday cake and making a wish? That is candle magick in action.

The purpose of this book is to introduce people to the powerful art of candle magick. No previous experience in any form of magick is necessary. The advantages it has over other forms of magick are considerable:

1. The rituals are simple, but effective.

2. The costs are minimal and the props can be made or bought anywhere.

3. There is no need for special robes and intricate ceremonies.

4. The rituals can be performed anywhere, indoors or out.

5. There is no need for years of training. Students can start right away, and enjoy quick results.

6. Candles are extremely versatile. Rituals can be used to attract, repel, protect, and divine the future.

Who Will Buy This Book?

The audience for this book are people who are interested in performing spells, rituals, and divinations on their own. They do not want to spend years learning obscure esoteric facts; they want to achieve results as quickly as possible.

This is a practical, how-to book, aimed at people who are either just beginning in magick, or who have already learned other aspects of the new age and want to learn something practical and useful. By the time they have finished reading this book they will know everything necessary to perform this powerful method of magick.

My Credentials

I have been involved in the world of magick virtually all of my life. My first experiments in candle magick were made while I was a teenager, and the success of these ensured my continuing interest in the subject. My experiences in candle magick are practical, rather than theoretical.

I used candle magick to help establish myself as a writer. I have written seventy-five books over the last thirty years, and make my living as a fulltime writer.

Market Analysis

My aim in writing this book is to teach people how to perform effective candle magick. I want them to understand how and why it works, and then be able to use it in their own lives. There are a number of other books on the subject in the marketplace, but none are as practical as I intend my book to be.

There are three "classic" books on the subject that continue to sell well, year after year. Two of these are by Dr. Raymond Buckland: *Practical Candleburning Rituals* and *Advanced Candle Magick* (both published by Llewellyn). The other is *The Master Book of Candle Burning* by Henri Gamache, which was first published in 1942. It covers the essentials well, but is aimed primarily at people interested in African-American candle burning.

One of two notable recent titles is: *The Candle Magick Book* by Kala and Ketz Pajeon (Citadel Press, 1991) which is a workbook on the subject, complete with exercises, tests, and places to write notes. It is informative, but not surprisingly reads more like a workbook than a book. It would make an excellent textbook. The other, *Wicca Candle Magick* by Gerina Dunwich (Citadel Press, 1997), is geared primarily toward Wiccan readers. It contains interesting spells, rituals and magick.

It is interesting to note that all of these books have enjoyed many printings, showing an increasing interest in the subject over the last sixty years.

In the last two years four new books have been published, all by well-known New Age authors. These are: *A Little Book of Candle Magic* by D. J. Conway (Freedom, Calif.: The Crossing Press, 2000), *Exploring Candle Magick: Candle Spells, Charms, Rituals and Divinations* by Patricia Telesco (Franklin Lakes, N.J.: Career Press, Inc., 2001), *Candle Power: Using Candlelight for Ritual, Magic and Self-Discovery* by Cassandra Eason (London: Blandford Press Ltd., 2000), and *Candle Magic: A Coveted Collection of Spells, Rituals and Magical Paradigms* by Phillip Cooper (York Beach, Maine: Red Wheel/Weiser, 2000). At first glance, it might appear that the field is becoming crowded, but these books are being published solely because of increasing public interest in candle magick. Naturally, to be viable, any new book would have to be different to the titles that are already available.

My book will be different to the others. It will be a book that people can read for pleasure, as well as for information. I hope it will become a reference book as well, but its primary purpose is to teach people how to use candle magick to achieve their goals.

There will be a great deal of original information in my book. The cosmic vibration method of timing, and the rituals for magic squares, have not appeared in print before. The angelic healing technique section contains material that is new and original. The two candle wax methods of divination are not covered in any books I have found on candle magick. I learned how to do this while living in Scotland in the 1960s. Dressing the candle with water, rather than oil, might be controversial, but is covered as an option for people who do not like using oils. I am not sure if this information has appeared in print before.

I have witnessed many candle magic rituals in the East where wax candles have been used for more than two thousand years. Colored candles were used in marriage ceremonies, and they were also used to measure periods of time. There is a great deal of sexual symbolism related to candles in the East. I do not think it would be worth including an entire chapter on the magickal uses of candles in the East, but will incorporate much of this material in the text.

Chapters

Introduction

The introduction will begin with my introduction to candle magick as a teenager. A friend of mine had been experimenting with candle magick, and was extremely enthusiastic about it. When I discussed a problem I was concerned about with him, he immediately suggested that I burn some candles. I thought the idea was crazy, and refused for awhile. However, the problem did not resolve itself, and finally I burned some candles. Much to my surprise, the candle magic worked.

Although I have used candle magick for different purposes at various times in my life, the other main personal example I will include is how I used candle magick to progress in my writing career.

The introduction continues with a brief history of fire, candles, and candle magick. Common examples of candle magick that people may not be aware of include candle burning in the Catholic church, blowing out candles on birthday cakes, belief in salamanders, etc. The festival of Candlemas shows that candles have been used in rituals from pre-Christian times.

Even today, many people believe that spirits like candles and are attracted to them. Consequently, it is believed that candles can help spiritual awareness, clairvoyance, and contact with deceased relatives.

There are a number of superstitions about candles that will be mentioned here. For instance, if the candle burns with a blue flame, it is a sign of a ghostly presence. When a candle sparks it means a letter is coming. Candles were lit at births, marriages, and deaths to ward off evil spirits, etc.

Chapter One: What Is Candle Magick?

Chapter One will start with a brief description of magick and what it can and cannot do. This will segue into candle magick, and how it can be used today to attract, repel, and protect. Examples will be given on how it can be used to attract love, money, and good health. It can also be used for divination. Examples will be given to illustrate each of these aspects of candle magick.

Candle magick can be deceptive. Because it is easy to do, people often overlook it. Yet it can be as powerful and useful as any other magickal technique.

The basic process consists of choosing the correct color candle, dressing it, consecrating it, and burning it. While doing these things, the participant needs to remain focused on his or her goal. While the candle is burning, energies go out into the universe to attract the participant's desires.

Some people use candle magick unconsciously. A friend of mine lights candles every Sunday night while journaling. She chooses candles that appeal to her at the time, and somehow they always relate to what is going on in her life. Suggestions will be given on how to do this consciously to improve the quality of the reader's life.

Chapter Two: Candles and Other Implements

All the main types of candles will be described in this chapter, along with suggestions on how to choose them and when each one should be used. Beeswax, altar, planetary, astral, offertory, and novena candles will all be covered.

In addition, spills or tapers, snuffers, oils, censers, incense, altars, candle holders, and pendulums will also be discussed. A pendulum might sound a trifle unusual in a book on candle magick, but it plays a valuable part in determining the correct candle to use, correct timing, and the value of the request.

Chapter Three: How to Make Your Own Candles

Full instructions will be given on how to make candles. The necessary implements will be described, followed by instructions on how to make dipped, rolled and molded candles. Instructions on how to make scented and/or multicolored candles for specific purposes will also be included.

To make the candles even more effective, there is a ritual of concentration that can be performed while making them. This will be explained in detail.

Chapter Four: Color

We all react to different colors, and color symbolism is an important aspect of candle magick. Most people in the West consider white to be pure and good, for instance, while black is considered negative and symbolic of the dark side. Consequently, it is important that the correct color candles be used, and these are determined by the desired goal.

The positive and negative traits of each color will be listed and described, followed by suggestions on how to choose the correct color.

Chapter Five: Fragrance

Different fragrances add power to your magickal aims, and should be selected carefully. This chapter will give advice on choosing fragrances that relate to the different planets, and the days of the week. Francis Barrett's magical fumes will be included, but for the most part, I will focus on pleasant fragrances.

It is a good idea to bathe before any ritual, and a fragrant magickal bath before undertaking candle magick is extremely beneficial. Advice will be given on how to do this to create the maximum effect.

The use of incense in candle burning will be discussed here also.

Chapter Six: How to Prepare a Candle

Once the candle has been made, it has to be dressed, charged, and consecrated for its purpose. Different oils can be used for different purposes, and advice will be given on how to choose the right oil for your candle. Instructions will be given on the correct way to dress the candle with oil. This will be followed by a ritual for charging your candle, and instructions will be given on how to consecrate your candle for its purpose.

Not everyone likes to use oils. I have met a number of people who find their scent nauseating. Consequently, I will include information on how to dress candles with water. I am not sure if this information has appeared in print before.

Chapter Seven: Timing

The right time to conduct a spell or ritual is extremely important. This chapter will provide advice on the best times using a number of methods. An ephemeris, almanac, or astrological calendar is useful in determining the Moon's phases, and the position of the Moon in each sign. Advice will be given on how to use these effectively.

The planetary hours, days of the week, and the time of birth are all effective methods, and will be taught in detail.

My own personal method of timing is to use the person's cosmic vibration from his or her day of birth. This has not appeared in print before.

I will also cover what to do if the person has an urgent need to burn candles for a specific purpose, but the timing is wrong. This is a common problem that is not discussed anywhere else.

Naturally, everyone wants quick results. Consequently, the final section of this chapter will cover when to expect results.

Chapter Eight: Numerology and Candles

Candles and numerology work well together. The Life path represents the person's purpose in life, the Expression reveals the natural abilities, and the Soul Urge shows the heart's desire. Candles can be used to help the person find his or her correct path in this lifetime. They can also be used for achieving various goals and for releasing karmic factors from previous lifetimes.

Chapter Nine: Magickal Alphabets

A major part of candle consecration involves inscribing the candles with symbols, or the desired goal. Symbols can be inscribed on candles openly, but frequently secret alphabets, such as Theban, Etruscan, and Templar, are used to keep the goal a secret.

This chapter discusses the various alphabets and methods of inscribing the goals on candles. It is also possible to write your goals on pieces of paper that are then placed underneath the candles. Another method is to write the goals on paper and then to burn it in the candle. How and when these should be done will be covered in this chapter.

Chapter Ten: Magick Squares

Magick squares have been used in magick for thousands of years. They originated in China and are still a major force in Asian magick (yantras) and in the Western magickal tradition. There is a magic square for each day of the week. These are drawn on parchment or paper on the correct day and then burned in the appropriate colored candle. For example, the Square of Jupiter would be burned in a green candle on a Thursday to achieve success in financial or business matters. The specific ritual for each day of the week will be included.

Chapter Eleven: Healing With Candles

Magick should be used to help others, and it would be hard to find anything more important than healing the sick. This chapter teaches how to involve the archangel Raphael in your candle-healing rituals. Other forms of healing using candles will also be included. The bulk of this chapter will be on healing people, ourselves as well as others, but a section will be included on healing pets and other animals.

Chapter Twelve: Candle Divination

Divination with candle wax is little known today. This chapter teaches the reader how to interpret the patterns candle wax makes in a container of water to divine the future and to answer questions. Two methods will be taught: a simple past, present, and future method to answer specific questions, and a more involved method that can provide a complete reading.

Smoke reading will also be covered. This is the art of interpreting the smudges created on a sheet of paper held over a candle.

The final part of this chapter will cover lychnomancy, the art of interpreting how the candle burns. Examples of this are: a rising or falling flame is a sign of danger, a dim flame shows that caution is required, and it is a sign of good luck if one of three candles burns more strongly than the others.

Chapter Thirteen: Candle Rituals

Finally, we come to the section that most people consider to be candle magick: spells and rituals. Detailed instructions, hints, and advice will be given on practical rituals for:

- Protection

- Achieving goals

- Relieving problems from past lives

- Releasing karma

- Attracting spirit guides and angel guardians

- Achieving happiness, success, prosperity, and love

Conclusion

The final chapter is intended to motivate the readers to action. They will now know the basics of candle magick, and how they can use it to help themselves and others. All they need do now is decide what they want, and then follow the specific instructions given in this book to achieve their goals using candle magick.

Suggested Reading

The book will contain a bibliography of books on candle magic, candle making, color, fragrances, healing, magic squares, and magick.

Index

An index will be included.

If I was sending this proposal to a publisher I would include a sample chapter—probably Chapter One, "What is Candle Magick?" as that provides a clear picture of what the book is all about.

It takes time to create a proposal of this sort, and I find it best to do it over a few days, rather than in one session. You will have noticed that this outline covers some of the information required in Llewellyn's guidelines. It can be helpful to at least partially complete Llewellyn's questions before starting to write your book. By doing this, you will clarify in your own mind exactly what you want to include in your book. You may decide to write a complete book proposal for yourself, even if it is not required by your publisher. This will tell you exactly what you will include in your book, as well as information on the market, competitive titles, and the strengths of your book. You will write a powerful book if you have a complete book proposal by your side. You will also write it more quickly.

A good friend of mine is busy writing a book purely because I encouraged him to write a proposal. He had been trying to get his fiction published for many years without success. I suggested that he write a book on model railways, as he is passionate about his hobby of playing with miniature trains. Over lunch we worked out the chapter headings, and then he created a complete proposal, which he sent to a publisher who specializes in books of this sort. He received a small advance, and is looking forward to having his first book published.

Incidentally, he has two more books on the subject already outlined. My friend is achieving success because he created a complete book proposal. You can do the same.

Your book is now outlined. It is now time to do whatever additional research is necessary before you start writing. That will be covered in the next chapter.

6

RESEARCH

Obviously, you need raw material with which to write your book. At least some of this will come from your research. Naturally, you will already know something about the subject you are intending to write about, but it would be remarkable if you could write an entire book without doing at least some research.

The ability to research effectively is a vital skill for any nonfiction writer. Even if you are the world's leading authority on a certain subject, you will still need to research facts and figures, to ensure that your finished book is as accurate as possible. I have written several books without doing any research beforehand, as I already knew enough about the subjects to write the first drafts. However, after writing these books, I referred to other books to ensure that my facts were correct.

Many writers prefer researching to writing. They enjoy discovering obscure facts about their subject and spend countless hours in libraries gathering information. In some cases, all this activity is an excuse not to write. The problem with doing too much research is that you ultimately have to sift through a huge pile of information to sort out the material you need. It is important to know when to stop researching.

In most cases, your outline will tell you when you've done enough research. Your outline pinpoints the areas of your topic that you are not an expert on. It can be helpful to write down a series of questions relating to these areas, and then research until you have enough material to comprehensively answer them.

There are two types of research sources: primary and secondary. A primary source is original information that you obtain through interviews, your own experiences, or from original personal papers, diaries, and other correspondence. Secondary sources are published materials, such as books, magazines, newspapers, and radio and television interviews. Naturally, primary sources are more valuable to you as a writer, as they enable you to incorporate material in your book that may not be available anywhere else.

Research can be done in a number of ways:

1. You can research other books. This means going to the library, or buying new or used books.

2. You can do research over the Internet.

3. You can interview people who are knowledgeable about the subject.

4. You can keep clipping files of articles in your areas of interest.

5. You can conduct experiments, or observe what is going on in your world.

| BOOKS

Books are the first things that people think of when talking about research. No matter what subject you intend writing about, you can be sure there are other books already published on the same, or similar, topic. You can use other books for information, but obviously you cannot copy pages of material from other books. This is the same as stealing, and is a breach of copyright. However, brief quotations can be considered "fair use." Naturally, you must credit the author for the quotation, and give full details of the book, author, and publisher. Llewellyn's guidelines are helpful in defining fair use. As "a rule of

thumb 200 words total quoted from a 300-page book or 50 words total from a periodical" is considered fair use.

You also do not want to simply paraphrase another author. This means that you are rewriting someone else's ideas and claiming them as your own. This is not fair. Your book must contain your own ideas. Consequently, use other books to check facts and to learn important information, but make sure that your book is your own.

I have a large reference library that is constantly growing, and recommend that you build up a collection of books and magazines that relate to your areas of interest. I am sure you are already doing this. Not only will your library become increasingly useful for research, it will also provide you with enormous pleasure. I also use five libraries in my city for research purposes. One of these is a university library, another is a Theosophical Society library, and the others are general libraries.

The reference section of your local library is often a good place to start your research. You may find some of the topics you are researching in the *Encyclopedia Britannica*, for instance. At the end of some of these articles is a list of sources that you can follow up.

There are other books in the Reference section that will also prove useful. One of these is *The Reader's Guide to Periodic Literature*. It lists by subject and author all the fiction and nonfiction published in 125 magazines since 1900. If you want to find out if a leading magazine has published anything on topics that interest you, you can look it up here. Even better, if your library belongs to FirstSearch, you have access to almost six million articles online, taken from seventy-five bibliographic data bases. If you are searching for articles published before 1900, refer to *Poole's Index to Periodical Literature*. This covers articles published from 1802 to 1906. (An online subscription service that provides access to 3,500 articles from 1770 is www.chadwyck.com.) There are many other indexes as well.

Naturally, you should also study the library catalog. This will be on a computer terminal nowadays. Do a search under as many subject

headings as possible. You will get ideas for these by looking at the page following the title page on books that relate to your topic. For instance, two subject headings are listed in my book *Write Your Own Magic*. They are: 1. Magic. 2. Success—Miscellanea. In *Feng Shui for Beginners*, Interior Decoration is listed as a subject heading. Another possibility is to study the index entries on other books that relate to your area of interest. You will also find it useful to examine the bibliography, preface, and acknowledgments for potential subject headings and books to seek out.

When researching in a library, I naturally borrow as many books as possible, so that I can study them at leisure. If I am interested in only a few lines from a book, I jot them down in a notebook. When doing this I make a note reminding me if I copied the words directly from the book, or if I paraphrased them. In either case, I record full details about the book.

If the book is in the reference section and I cannot borrow it, I will either make notes in my notebook or take photocopies of the relevant pages. Again, it is important to keep a complete record of where the information came from.

Make friends with librarians in all of the libraries you use. They are knowledgeable, helpful people who will be happy to direct you to the right books or data banks. In my experience, they enjoy helping authors, and frequently go out of their way to provide valuable information.

I also spend a great deal of time in new and used bookstores, searching for books that will be useful to me. Although I love browsing in used bookstores, it is usually quicker to find out-of-print books through the Internet. Bookfinder.com is just one of the many excellent sites you can go to on the net when searching for books. I have also bought many out-of-print books through Amazon.com. Although they are primarily known for new books, their used book business is growing rapidly.

One author I know buys all the used books she can find on the subject of her current book. She then resells them once she has finished writing her own book. This is a good way of cutting down the costs of research, and might be an idea you can utilize. It would be impossible for me to do this. Once I buy a book, it becomes a friend and I am extremely reluctant to part with it. My wife is always telling me to decrease the size of my library, claiming that some of the books have not been opened in years. This is true, but who knows when I'll desperately need a particular book? I am always buying books, but seldom part with any of them.

Another way of obtaining books that might be useful for research purposes is to become a book reviewer for a specialist magazine. Not only will you receive free books, but in some cases you will be paid as well.

One author I know writes to publishers asking for free copies of books on similar topics to the one he is currently writing. He explains that he will recommend these books to his readers in the bibliography. Apparently, this idea works, but I would rather buy my own copies of books, as I would hate to be obliged to recommend a book that I did not think was a valuable work on the subject.

| THE INTERNET

I got on to the Internet early, as I thought it would be a wonderful tool for research. Unfortunately, although it is getting better, it has been a major disappointment so far. There are huge amounts of material on every esoteric subject you could think of on the Internet, but much of it is rubbish. If you type in, say, "telepathy," thousands of pages will become available to you. You have to sort through all the pages that are advertising services or products, and read the pages that are ostensibly articles about telepathy. However, here you will have to use your judgment. Anyone can put up a page on any topic they wish. Consequently, you have to search through an incredible amount of dross in the hope of finding a particle of gold. I find that I can spend hours surfing the net, admittedly having a good time, but at the end have less information than I would have gained from a trip to the library.

The leading exceptions to this are the Internet sites run by reputable magazines and newspapers, such as *The New York Times.* Obviously, the quality of material from sites of this sort is likely to be far more reliable than information you get from a site you know nothing at all about. Browsing through the archives of magazines and newspapers online can be an effective way of gaining ideas for articles of your own.

Another exception is theMYSTICA.com, an Internet encyclopedia, which is growing rapidly and contains a large number of useful articles on the New Age. In time, there will be more resources of this quality on the web.

The Internet is a valuable tool when used with caution. Fortunately, there are now a number of books available to help you research on the web.[1] Use the Internet for research, but evaluate the information you find there carefully.

| PEOPLE

I find this to be the most useful method of research when writing New Age books. Everyone has a story to tell, and most people are happy to talk about what they know if approached in the right way. Of course, what they tell you still has to be checked out.

Twenty-five years ago, when I was traveling up and down the Pacific Rim on a regular basis, I spoke to hundreds of people about feng shui, a subject that was little known in the West at the time. Most people answered my questions honestly, but some deliberately tried to mislead me with false information. They were doing this because feng shui was important to them, and they did not want it to get into the hands of ignorant Westerners. Their motives were good, but it caused me a great deal of confusion and wasted huge amounts of time. Although it was frustrating, it taught me the importance of checking everything.

Over the last thirty years, almost everyone I wanted to interview has been happy to help. Many people are flattered to think that I sought them out. Some people welcome the exposure that mention of their name in a book or magazine article will give them. After all, what is the use of being an expert, if no one knows about it?

Experts are not always easy to find. However, you will be able to find leads in *The Directory of Directories* (Detroit, Michigan: Gale Research Company), which can be found in any large library. This book contains lists of specialized directories in many different subject areas. You can also ask New Age bookstores for the names of knowledgeable people in your area. If your area supports a regional New Age newspaper or magazine, you can contact the authors of different articles that relate to your areas of interest. It also pays to look at the advertisements to see if any of the practitioners would be able to help you. These people are usually thrilled to be interviewed, as any exposure helps to promote whatever it is that they are doing.

... everyone has a story to tell ...

Public relations companies will be happy to help you find experts. After all, their job is to promote their clients, and if you can help them do it, they will be happy to give you names and contact details.

There are also some Internet sites that will help you find experts. Profnet.com, NewsWise.com, and Experts.com all have searchable data bases of experts on a wide range of topics. GuestFinder.com is another good source of interesting people to interview.

You must be organized before interviewing anyone. Prepare a list of questions. This means you must know what you want to achieve from the interview ahead of time. Naturally, other questions will occur to you while you are interviewing the subject, but you need a list of important questions, both to provide the answers you need, and to demonstrate that you have done your homework beforehand.

Make an appointment. It is inconsiderate to simply turn up without an appointment and expect to be allowed an interview. An appointment also gives your subject time to think about the interview, and it provides you with time to research your subject and think of the questions you want to ask.

Naturally, you must arrive punctually for your appointment. I aim to be in the area about twenty minutes early. This means that I can still arrive on time, even when held up by traffic. I am happy to park down the road for a while, if necessary. This gives me time to think about the interview, and I arrive without feeling stressed or flustered.

I use a notebook and three cassette recorders. I am sure I could manage with two, but I use three to make absolutely sure that the interview will be recorded successfully on at least one of them. I used to use two cassette recorders. One day I turned up at someone's home to conduct an interview, and placed both recorders on his desk. My subject had never been interviewed before and was nervous. Throughout the interview, he drummed his fingers underneath the desk. I was not aware of this at the time. When I listened to the tapes, most of it was incomprehensible, because all I could hear was his nervous tapping. That taught me a lesson. As well as encouraging me to invest in a third machine, I started placing them on different surfaces to eliminate any possibility of a repeat of the drumming incident. I also use fresh batteries and good quality cassettes. I take plenty of spare batteries and cassettes with me to every interview.

Because some people are intimidated by recorders, my machines are as small and insignificant looking as possible. While setting them up, I tell my subject that I will be recording the conversation to ensure that any direct quotations I use will be correct, and so I won't have to keep stopping to take notes.

I take as much time as necessary to relax my subject before starting the interview. Some people are shy and need to be encouraged to speak. On the other hand, of course, some people hardly give you a chance to ask your questions. Interviewing is a skill that takes time to master. You need to encourage quiet people to open up and answer questions in reasonable detail. You also need to guide the chatty ones in the direction you want the interview to go. Do not talk too much yourself. The whole point of the interview is to record your subject's thoughts and ideas. Ideally, you want your subject to open up and talk, rather than simply answer questions. I find brief pauses after my subject has stopped speaking encourage him or her to start talking again. I smile and nod my head a great deal as well, to gently encourage my subject to keep talking.

I begin by discussing the topic of the interview and my reasons for requesting it. I then start asking questions. I have a notebook on my lap and occasionally jot down a quick note. I keep this to an absolute minimum, as I do not want my subject to stop talking while I take notes. The notes I write down usually relate to topics my subject has raised that I want to ask further questions about, but do not want to interrupt the flow of conversation right away. I also make quick notes about the décor of the room, the type of clothes my subject is wearing, how confident or nervous he or she is, and so on. It is unlikely that I will need any of this information, but it is useful background material that might be helpful to know later on.

At the end of the interview, I thank my subject and leave as quickly as possible, without appearing rude or unduly hasty. This is because I want to listen to the cassettes and write up the interview while it is still fresh in my mind. I always send a thank-you note to anyone who has been kind enough to let me interview them. If the interview has been particularly useful to me, I will also send them a copy of the book once it has been published. If I mention someone's name in a book, I also always send him or her a copy.

Sometimes your subjects will want to see what you write about the interview, in order to verify it. I have no objection to sending them a copy of what I have written. Occasionally, they will offer new material at this stage, and this can prove useful.

Naturally, many of your interviews will be done over the phone. The same rules apply. Have a prepared list of questions ready before you phone, just in case the person asks to be interviewed there and then. Ask your subject's permission to record the interview before starting. Some people prefer a phone interview to a personal one. They might be busy or would rather you did not visit in person.

Sometimes you can interview people by e-mail or mail. Always ask permission first. Never send a list of questions to anyone without asking. Remember to enclose a stamped self-addressed envelope for your subject's reply. You should also send an e-mail or letter back to thank them once you receive their responses. (Sadly, this is rare. I am frequently interviewed by e-mail and seldom receive a thank you.) If you are asking a number of people the same questions, you might choose to send a questionnaire to each of them. This is not as friendly or as personal as a letter or e-mail, and the replies are likely to be briefer. However, it might be all that is required. When sending out a questionnaire to a number of people, always ask at the end if they have any further comments they would like to make. This can be a rich source of material.

I dislike talking in detail about my books while I am working on them. However, I have found it helpful to tell people the subject matter of whatever book it is I am working on. Every now and again, someone will give me useful information, or provide an introduction to someone else who knows something about the topic. Some years ago, while writing *Dowsing for Beginners*, I told a friend about the project. I knew that he had served in Vietnam, but had no idea that he had used dowsing rods there. Naturally, the information he gave me appeared in the book.

Sometimes you need background information, rather than expert knowledge. If, for example, you know a great deal about the history and meanings of the runes, but have never given readings for others with them, you might have conversations with professional rune readers to gain insight into how and why they do the things they do. You do not need a world authority on the runes for this. Any competent professional reader would be able to give you the information you require.

Teaching classes is another excellent way of gaining information. I taught classes for many years, and after each lesson almost always wrote notes about something unexpected or interesting that had occurred. I took these notes for my own interest, but many of them have appeared in my books.

Everyone has a story to tell. Be alert to opportunity everywhere you go. Carry a notebook with you. You will be amazed at the number of things you write down that would otherwise be forgotten.

| Clipping Files

You will find it helpful to keep clippings of newspaper and magazine articles that relate to your areas of interest. I keep my clippings in boxes that are clearly labeled by subject area. A friend of mine keeps her clippings in a filing cabinet. It makes no difference how you store them, just as long as you can find the information when you need it.

Make sure that you record on the clipping where it came from, along with the dates, section of the paper or magazine it came from, and the name of the author.

Of course, magazine articles frequently start near the front of the magazine and then continue in the back sections. If you cut these out, you run the risk of losing sections of other articles that may be of interest later on. One remedy is to photocopy the articles that interest you. An alternative is to file the entire magazine. If you are using a filing cabinet, you can file notes in the relevant positions to remind you which magazine the article can be found in.

| Observation and Experimentation

We all question things as we go through life. Your book might be based on the results of your thoughts, meditations, experiments, and observations. This is primary research at its best, and the information in your book will be fresh and innovative.

You need to be careful with this form of research. Too often, people come up with ideas and then make enormous leaps of logic to arrive at conclusions that are tenuous, to say the least. Here is an example. I love the works of William Shakespeare. As part of this interest, I have also read many books about Shakespeare, the man, and at least as many more from people who claim that Shakespeare did not write the plays he is credited with. I particularly enjoy these books. However, the lengthy arguments, expounding the virtues of different candidates, invariably end up with far too many suppositions for me to accept them.

Original experimentation is good, as long as the reader is told what it is. If you discovered a new way to reach the astral plane, I would be interested in reading about it. However, I would also want to know that you invented the method, the success rate you had had with it, and if anyone else had been able to astral travel using your method.

Observation and experimentation are useful methods that will help make your book different to anything else on the market.

| OTHER RESOURCES

You can use the Internet to explore the different databases and news groups that relate to your areas of interest. You will find a mixture of good, bad, and downright crazy information among the news group messages, but they can also help you determine what your audience is looking for. You can waste incredible amounts of time wading through the different news groups, so try not to become involved in endless discussions with people who have nothing better to do than post lengthy articles on news groups.

You can also employ people to do the research for you. I cannot imagine ever doing that myself, as I love researching my books. However, if you are incredibly busy, or do not enjoy hunting down information, you can employ an information broker to search for you. You can find these people through the Yellow Pages, the Internet, or by asking at a good library. Another alternative is to hire a college student to research for you. The main problem I see in employing someone else to do your research is that although they may find a wealth of material, they may overlook the small, intriguing snippets of information that help make your book fresh and different.

| HELPFUL HINTS

Collecting huge amounts of information can be intimidating. This becomes less of a problem if you classify the material as you obtain it. This can also save you a great deal of time when you write the book. You might want to have a file folder or box for each chapter. The material can be safely stored there until you start working on the chapter. I keep a sheet of paper in each folder on which I record where to find information that cannot conveniently be stored inside it. This might be relevant page numbers from particular books, or perhaps a cassette of a particular interview.

I also find it useful to make extensive notes as I research. I might summarize the information I gain from a certain book to make sure that I understand it. I might ask myself questions about the material, and then try to answer them.

While researching, I keep in mind the information my readers will want to learn from the book. This stops me from wasting too much time exploring topics that might be fascinating but will, at best, warrant only a brief mention in the book.

| RESEARCHING THROUGH LIFE

As you are obviously interested and involved in the psychic world you are probably researching all the time, even though you may not call it that. Every time you attend a class or workshop, read a book or magazine, or talk with like-minded people, you are gaining information. It is a good habit to make notes of interesting facts that you learn as you go through life, and record these in a journal, diary, or notebook.

I have kept notebooks for more than thirty years and have thousands of pages of notes relating to almost every psychic subject you could think of. While living in Cornwall more than thirty years ago, I became friendly with a group of Gypsies who taught me how to use a crystal ball. I still have the notes I made about this. While in Singapore in the late 1960s, I was introduced to feng shui. Almost thirty years later, the notes I made then became the basis of several books. While in India, I recorded hundreds of pages of notes about the Kartikeyan system of palmistry. This system, which is hundreds of years old, examines 153 minor lines that can be found on the hand. I may decide to write a book about this one day. While working in the Far East I accidentally heard someone mention animal dreaming. This is a belief that if a woman dreams of a certain animal shortly before conceiving, the child will exhibit the properties of the particular animal.

... carry a notebook and make a habit of taking notes ...

Researching this took months, but I have a couple of notebooks full of information that I learned. Again, this might one day form the basis of a book. In the United States I met a fascinating woman who gave smoke readings. She held a sheet of paper over a candle and then interpreted the smudge marks from the soot. It was fascinating to watch her do this, and I have pages of information about the art that I learned from her. As a teenager, I watched a friend achieve a specific goal by burning certain candles. Asking him questions about this started a life-long interest in the subject. I have hundreds of pages of notes on candle burning that I have recorded over the last thirty-five years. These are just a few examples from my notebooks.

Sometimes the notes are brief. One example is my meeting with a banana reader. Several years ago, in London, I came across a man who read banana peels. He worked every weekend in a market. People would buy a banana, eat it, and then give him the peel to interpret. He gave amazingly insightful readings from the specific bananas people bought, and from the way in which they peeled them. I bought him lunch when he finished and enjoyed learning about his unusual talent. I probably would have forgotten this incident if I hadn't recorded a couple of paragraphs about it in my notebook.

I recorded this information for my own interest, and now have dozens of exercise books full of esoteric information that I have picked up over the years. I still do this everywhere I go. Whenever I travel, an exercise book is the first item to be packed, as I never know what I might discover.

None of this information was ever recorded with the intention of publishing it at a later date. All I did was write down the things that interested me at the time. If you get into the habit of doing this, you will be amazed at the amount of fascinating material you collect. By doing this, you will never run out of topics to write about. Browsing through your notebooks will give you ideas for books and articles, and you will have at your fingertips information that is possibly not available anywhere else.

Naturally, you should keep all of your research material, as you might decide to write another book or some magazine articles on the same subject at a later date. I keep mine with my clipping files. This means that I can add additional material whenever I find it. For instance, I am not planning to write another book on auras at this stage, but a few weeks ago I read an interesting article on how auras are being used to reveal people's predisposition towards different diseases. I carefully cut it out and placed it in my "Aura" box, where it is available for use at any time in the future.

7
WRITING YOUR BOOK

Creating an outline may seem like a huge amount of work. However, it will enable you to write the book more quickly and with less effort than if you had turned on your computer, and started writing with no previous forethought. Thanks to your outline, you have a good idea about what is going to be covered in each chapter. You know what you are going to write about. You have all the material you need. Now it is time to start. Think about the imaginary person you are writing the book for, and put pen to paper, or fingers on keyboard.

| PREPARING TO WRITE

People vary in how they start writing a book. I am extremely good at delaying the start, but, once I have a few words down on paper, I am able to keep working at it until the book is finished. A friend of mine tidies her house before starting work on a new book. This spring cleaning effectively allows her to forget about any more housework until her book is finished. Another acquaintance takes this a step further. He has his car serviced, gets his e-mails and other correspondence up to date, enjoys spending time with all of his friends, and then becomes a hermit for the length of time it takes to complete the book. An attendee at one of my *Wake Up and Write!* seminars told me that she carefully chooses and buys a new pen with which to write the first draft of her book.

These people are all preparing to write. It is a process that most writers seem to go through. Finally, though, they settle down and start to write.

| THE FIRST SENTENCE

The first sentence can be a stumbling block for many writers. Plato is reputed to have written the first sentence of *The Republic* fifty times. The would-be author who told me this was alarmed because he thought that if Plato needed fifty attempts, he had no hope of ever starting a book. I saw it differently. The first sentence does not have to be perfect the first time, as you can always go back, as Plato did, and change it. You want the first sentence to be as powerful and as enticing as possible. However, it does not have to be perfect on the first draft as you can always change it, fifty or more times if you wish, when you revise the book. Get that first sentence down on paper, and then keep on writing.

| FINDING TIME

Writing a book takes a considerable amount of time and effort. The most sensible way to write a book is to work at it steadily, following a regular schedule. Ideally, write something every day. It does not matter how much or how little you produce, just as long as some progress is made every time you sit down at your computer. You might decide to write five hundred or a thousand words a day. Perhaps you would rather complete one page or three pages every day. You might choose to write for thirty or sixty minutes every day. It does not matter how modest your daily requirement is. If you do this every day, you will ultimately finish the book. One page of double-spaced manuscript is about 250 words. If you write just one page every day, a 60,000-word book will be written in 240 days, which is only two-thirds of a year.

The important part is to establish a regular working routine, and then keep at it. I have abandoned a few books over the years by not sticking to a routine. We all lead busy lives, and it is easy to skip a day or two, and then a week. Before long, the book is put aside, and it is unlikely that it will be worked on again. Routine, and a small amount of discipline, is required.

You may even feel sorry for yourself while sitting in the bedroom in front of your computer while the rest of the family are watching a comedy on television. You hear the canned laughter, and before you know it, you are sitting on the sofa watching it with the rest of the family. It is important that you feel positive about your writing, and this is largely a mindset. Writing must become an important priority in your life. Years ago I heard an opera singer being interviewed on the radio. The interviewer said, "Poor you. You've got to go out and work tonight." The diva gave a wonderful reply. "Oh, no," she said. "Tonight I get to sing."

You have to approach your writing sessions in the same frame of mind. You may find it helpful to enjoy a leisurely shower or bath first, physically and symbolically getting rid of the stresses and tensions of the day. You might enjoy a brisk—or a leisurely—walk before settling down to your writing. Doing something like this separates your writing from everything else you have already done during the day. It gives you time to think about what you will be writing, so that when you sit down you will be relaxed and ready to start. And then you get to write.

Some authors write a letter or two before starting their serious writing. This can be helpful, and serves as a sort of warmup for the writing session ahead. Use it to get yourself started, if necessary, but do not become so lost in your correspondence that you neglect to work on your book. I used to read and answer my e-mails before starting to write. Unfortunately, the volume of e-mails has increased so dramatically that I can no longer do this. I check my e-mails to see if there is anything important, and read the others after I have finished my day's work.

I have already mentioned that I usually write 2,000 words a day. If the book I am working on is going to be approximately 60,000 words long, I know that the first draft will take thirty days to write. I mark that date in my diary to provide motivation. I then start writing and try to finish the first draft before the date that I've marked in my diary. It's a goal-setting game I play with myself. I'm delighted if I finish the first draft a day or two ahead of target, but I'm not concerned if I finish late. Obviously, the different things that occur in everyday life interfere with my schedule from time to time. Naturally, I attend to any important matters that crop up, but return to my writing as quickly as possible afterward.

Almost everyone complains about lack of time. However, if writing a book is important to you, you will find the time somehow. You may not be able to write every day. In fact, you may not be able to write at all during the week. Many people write their books during the weekends. Some authors get up early in the morning and write before starting their normal day. Anthony Trollope is an excellent example of someone who wrote dozens of books this way. Some people write late at night, once the family have gone to bed. I began writing by watching less television. This gave me the time I needed to write. I have never regretted missing any television programs because of my writing.

Writing is a solitary, time-consuming process that will affect your family at times, and may cause frustrations and difficulties. A meal out, or an evening at the movies, can be a useful way to thank your loved ones for their patience and understanding. It can also be a motivating factor for you. You should reward yourself in small ways whenever you achieve something.

| WRITERS WRITE

Of course, once you have made time to write, you must use it profitably. Writers write. You can think about your writing while traveling to and from work, or while waiting in line somewhere. You will be amazed at the number of spare moments you have during the day that can be put to good, productive use thinking about your book. Do the thinking then, and use your precious writing time to put words on paper.

Remain confident and positive. Many would-be authors become despondent and give up because they feel their writing is not perfect. This is the last thing you should worry about while writing the first draft. You will never achieve perfection, anyway. Write the very best that you can, and keep on writing until the book is finished. When you reread it, you will probably find that your writing is better than you thought it was. Any problems in your writing can be corrected when you revise the book. Concentrate on getting your first draft written. Once you have words on paper you can edit them, rearrange them or rewrite them, but get the words written first.

Some authors write a chapter, or even just a page, and then edit it. I find it much better to write the entire book before even thinking about editing anything. I seldom read through what I have previously written until after the first draft is completed.

Do not stop every time you get stuck, or need to research something. Write a note to yourself that further information needs to be added, and then keep on writing. You can look up the missing information and add it later. The most important thing to focus on with the first draft is putting words on paper.

Most writers experience doubt at some stage during the first draft, usually shortly after the half-way mark. They wonder why anyone would ever bother to read what they have written. They worry if their book will be good enough to get published, or if it will bore anyone crazy enough to read it.

You will probably experience this self-doubt while writing your own book. Realize that it is perfectly natural. Writing a book takes time and a great deal of hard work. When the words flow easily, writing is fun and enormously satisfying. However, it is not always, or even often, like this. It is when you are struggling with the sheer hard slog of writing that you experience self-doubt. You need to grit your teeth and keep on writing when this occurs. You might say to yourself that you are writing the book for you, and you do not care if anyone else ever reads it. Remember that this stage always passes. You might feel that you are wasting your time persevering with something that is unpublishable, but once you pass this point the writing will become pleasurable again, and you will gather momentum as you near the finish.

Of course, you may get stuck for other reasons. You might be tired or fed up with the whole process of writing. Have a rest if you are tired. I find it helpful to go for a walk or have a swim when I get bogged down in my writing. Sometimes I'll arrange to meet a friend for lunch or a cup of coffee. I try to forget about the book while I am out of the house, and almost always when I return I can get straight back into my writing again with new enthusiasm.

One of the members of my Master Mind group finds that all he needs to do when he gets stuck is to move to another room in the house. However, he writes longhand in an exercise book, which makes it easy for him to write anywhere. You could wander around the house if you were writing on a laptop, but I prefer to do my writing in my writing room, so his method does not work for me. However, it might for you.

Reward yourself in some way when you've finished the first draft. You have achieved something incredibly worthwhile. Celebrate. Go out for dinner. Throw a party. Have a vacation. Put your manuscript aside for a while and do something different. I have heard many authors say that completing the first draft of any book is the most satisfying aspect of being a writer.

Forget about your book for at least a week. A month would be even better. This will enable you to look at it again with fresh eyes when you start revising it.

| PROBLEMS

Writing a book is not a simple process, and almost everyone experiences problems along the way. How important the book is to you will largely determine whether or not you overcome the difficulties and finally produce a finished book. Sheer determination works for some people. One author I know considers it a matter of pride that she completes everything she starts. Toward the end of most of her books she puts aside all thoughts of publication, because she considers the book unpublishable, but she finishes it anyway. Then, after a week or two, she reads it and discovers that it was much better than she had thought while writing it.

| WRITER'S BLOCK

Writer's block is a common problem. The author sits down to write and finds that no words come. This occurs most frequently to people who fail to outline, but it can hit anyone. (This is yet another argument for outlining your book.) My solution is to put the manuscript to one side for an hour or two and do something completely different. I will probably go for a walk or swim. I might jump rope for a while, or visit a friend. While doing this I do not consciously think about the book, but when I return, the words usually start to flow again. If I continue having trouble after returning to my book, I temporarily abandon the section I am working on, and start another chapter. There is no law that states that you have to start at the introduction and work your way through to the conclusion. You can write the book in any order that suits you. By doing this, I find that when I return to the troublesome chapter a day or two later, the problem will have resolved itself.

| BOREDOM

Boredom is another problem, and can be a cause of writer's block. It may sound strange to discover that you can become bored when writing a book on a subject you love. However, it does happen. It can be hard to explain something that you know how to do in terms that other people will be able to understand. Sometimes you have to write down large amounts of basic information that are essential to the reader's understanding of the book. Although the topic of the book is exciting to you, the considerable amount of time you need to spend writing about the details of the subject can become boring.

I handle this by writing these parts in small doses. I might start my daily schedule by spending five or ten minutes working on one of these areas, and then move on to something that is more exciting. By doing this every day until the tedious part is over, I can spend most of my time writing about things that intrigue me, but still get the heavy-going part completed.

| FEAR

Fear can paralyze authors and stop the creative flow. A common fear is to think that your book is not good enough and no one would ever want to publish it. This is a form of perfectionism. The remedy is to temporarily forget about publication, and write the book for you.

| INTERRUPTIONS

Interruptions can be another problem. Some authors I know welcome interruptions as a distraction from the hard task of writing. Others refuse to answer their phones while they are writing. How you handle interruptions is up to you, but you need to ensure that you are left with enough time to write. Your family and friends might resent the amount of time you are spending on your book, and deliberately interrupt your work. Children and animals are another problem. You need tact in dealing with difficulties of this sort.

| STARTING A SESSION

Some writers find it hard to get going once they sit down for a writing session. I find it helpful to read the last page or two I wrote, and then carry on from there. A number of writers finish off their sessions in midsentence. When they return the next day, they finish that sentence and keep on writing. I usually jot down a few words on a scrap of paper before finishing to remind myself of where I am going. When I read this, the thoughts come back to me, and I'm able to start where I left off.

| DEVELOPING A ROUTINE

Most authors start their books with a burst of enthusiasm. After a while this begins to lag, and some people become bogged down with the daily grind of writing. Fortunate authors work through this, develop a routine, and find that they can't imagine life without sitting down to write every day. For others, it becomes harder and harder to write.

The remedy for this is to walk away from the book for a day, a week, or even a month. You might have been overly ambitious about the number of words you would produce every day. You may have set an impossible finishing date for your first draft. These goals are intended to motivate you, not hold you back.

Fortunately, you can change them. It doesn't matter if the book takes longer to finish than you originally thought. You might be able to write 500 words a day comfortably, but find 1,000 a major chore. Write the 500, and then enjoy the rest of the day. The book will take twice as long to write, but so what?

| FOOD

Eating can be a problem for many authors. As soon as they get stuck they start eating. Authors spend half their lives sitting down anyway, which means that excess food turns to fat. The remedy for this is to write with a glass of water nearby. When you get stuck, or have to stop to think, drink some water. I have heard water described as "brain food." I have no idea if this is true or not, but as I sip it I remind myself that I am providing my brain with nutrients that will help me come up with good ideas. The downside of drinking gallons of water is that you have to pay regular visits to the bathroom. This can also be seen as a good thing, though, as it forces you to get off your chair and move around.

I am a great believer in exercise for writers, anyway, because our work is so sedentary. I may or may not think about my writing while exercising, but either way I find that the words start flowing again as soon as I return to my desk.

| FINDING THE RIGHT WORDS

It can be frustrating to know exactly what you want to say, but be unable to express these thoughts in words on paper. There are two remedies for this that I have found helpful. The first is to write the difficult section in the form of a letter to a friend. You are more inclined to relax and let the words flow when you are writing an informal letter to a friend than you when you are writing a book that you hope will be read by thousands of people. The other remedy is to imagine your friend is sitting with you, and tell him or her about it. I prefer to speak out loud when doing this. After explaining the subject in either of these ways, I find the words flow freely once I return to my book.

| You Can Do It

Some days I can sit down and write two thousand words effortlessly. Other days it is a struggle. Every writer experiences this. If it was consistently easy, I doubt if I would still be writing, as all the challenge would go out of it. I find it interesting though, that when I read my finished manuscript I can not tell which sections were easy to write and which sections were difficult.

I can guarantee that you will have problems along the way. Every writer does. Keep on top of your thinking. Constantly tell yourself that you are a successful author. Visualize yourself in your favorite bookstore looking at a pile of books with your name on them. Picture yourself autographing books for an excited gathering of people. You would not have bought this book unless you wanted to become a writer. If you are committed to writing your book you will face all the problems that come your way, and overcome them.

8

REVISING YOUR BOOK

Revising your book should be an enjoyable and satisfying exercise. You will return to your manuscript with mixed feelings. Take pride in the fact that you have written a book, even though it is not finished yet. Spending time away from your book is a necessary part of the writing process. It allows you the necessary objectivity to look at your manuscript in a detached manner, as if you were the reader, rather than the writer. I prefer to revise my books in stages.

| STAGE ONE: READ AND MAKE NOTES

Read the book from start to finish, changing as little as possible. I find it helpful to print the book out, rather than read it on my computer screen. The purpose of this quick reading is to see if the book flows from start to finish. You might decide that some of the material in chapter seven would work better if placed in chapter five. Do not shift anything around while doing this first reading. Make a note of anything that you feel should be done, and carry on reading.

On this first reading you should also reassure yourself that you have written the book at the right level for your intended audience. You don't want a beginner's introduction to the psychic world to read like a university text, for instance. Make sure that you have adequately explained any terms that might be unfamiliar to your readers. Of course, the opposite situation can also occur. If you were writing an advanced book on the tarot, for instance, you would not need to explain what the major arcana was. You need to keep your intended reader just as much in mind when you are revising as you do when you are writing.

You will experience different reactions as you read through your book. In your imagination you probably thought that you had created a masterpiece. Consequently, you might feel disappointed at what you have written. There is no need to feel disheartened. All first drafts need revision before they are ready to be submitted to a publisher. That's why it's called a "first" draft. In fact, you will probably discover that parts of your book are better than you thought, while other parts need work.

| STAGE TWO: MAKE CHANGES

Read the book again, more slowly this time. Make any changes that you consider necessary. Now is the time to move material around, correct any errors, and make any additions or amendments. Take your time with this. You may have to rewrite sentences, paragraphs, or even chapters. Look for ambiguities, inconsistencies, and repetitions. Replace long words with short ones to make it easier to read, and ensure that what you have written is totally clear.

Keep an eye out for unintentional sexism. You might have to rephrase some sentences, or rewrite them in the plural, to avoid using "he" or "him," when you mean "he and she" or "him and her."

Check everything for accuracy. A friend of mine wrote a book on how to make a stone circle to predict the weather.[1] Although he had constructed dozens of these in the past, he still made another one, following the instructions in his book, to ensure that everything he had written was correct.

Almost all writers overwrite on their first drafts. See how many words you can eliminate without affecting the meaning. Be ruthless with adverbs and adjectives. This tightens your writing and gives it strength. You have to be careful with this, though. Eliminate any words that are not needed, but do not hesitate to add words, when necessary. A friend of mine likens himself to a sculptor when he is revising. He says that he chips away at everything that is not necessary, until he reveals the real book that is hiding inside.

| STAGE THREE: READ YOUR BOOK OUT LOUD

Once you feel that you have uncovered your real book, read it out loud. Do this with expression, pausing at all the commas and periods. You will be amazed at how clumsy some of your sentences appear when read out loud. Correct anything that you find. John Steinbeck went even further. He wrote his books in longhand and then dictated them to a tape recorder. He found that he picked up numerous errors while listening to the tapes.[2] You want your readers to learn from your books, but they should also enjoy reading them. Making any necessary changes while reading your work out loud makes your writing easier to read. People who read it will find your books friendly and conversational. This means they will enjoy learning whatever it is you are teaching them.

There is enormous satisfaction in rewriting, and some authors prolong this stage indefinitely. I sometimes wonder if these authors are secretly scared of rejection. As long as they keep revising their books, they do not have to send them to prospective publishers. Actually, no book is ever really finished—you could play around with your words forever. However, sooner or later you have to read it one last time, before getting it ready to submit to a publisher.

| FINAL STEPS

You may feel that honing and refining your prose is all that is required in the revision process. This is not entirely the case. You will need to draw up a table of contents, a bibliography, and an index. An index is a useful addition to any nonfiction book, and is virtually essential if you want to attract library sales. You may want to include a glossary, dedication page, and notes to enable readers to check your sources.

You can use your computer to create an index for you. I prefer to prepare the index while reading the book from start to finish for the last time. I use a printed-out copy of the manuscript and type the necessary words directly into my computer. This takes longer than having the computer do the indexing for me, but enables me to read the book yet again before sending it to my publisher. Think about your potential readers and what they would most want to know while you are working on your index. Create an index that is in proportion to the size of the book. A twenty-page index would look ridiculous in an eighty-page book, for instance. Similarly, an index listing a hundred references would be inappropriate in a book containing three or four hundred thousand words.

Even if I do not include notes in my book, which is extremely rare, I still keep a record of them to enable me to check any queries that my editors, or ultimately readers, ask. In practice, I prefer to include them in the book. I enjoy following up the sources listed in other people's books, and want my readers to be able to do the same with my books.

A glossary is essential if your book contains a large number of words and terms that the reader may not be familiar with. Even readers who know the terms will be interested in reading your definitions. If in doubt, include a glossary.

Have a final look at your title and subtitle. Naturally, it has to explain what the book is about. Ideally, your title should sound exciting, and intrigue the person in the publisher's acquisitions department who opens your parcel. However, it also needs to be appropriate for the book. *Feng Shui for Beginners* tells prospective readers exactly what the book is about. Consequently, it is a good title, even though it may not be an exciting one. Your publisher may well change the final title, anyway, but you should still aim to submit your book with the most appropriate title you can come up with.

Once all of these things have been done, read the book one last time, then print it out and send it on its way.

How to Prepare Your Submission Package

Your manuscript and cover letter are the first things that the people in the acquisitions department see. The package you send in has to look as professional as possible. If you were going to visit your publisher for the first time, you would naturally pay attention to your appearance. Your manuscript has to fulfill that task for you.

There are two types of submission packages. You can send in your complete manuscript, or you can send in a book proposal. Good presentation is vital for both. A handwritten book proposal will not even be looked at, and a letter full of misspelled words will likewise work against you. You may think that this does not happen, but in a novel-writing competition I judged recently, one entry was handwritten, and another had been typed on an old manual typewriter on what appeared to be rice paper. Most of the letters were filled in and the manuscript was virtually unreadable. These might have been prize-winning entries, if we had been able to read them.

| Your Manuscript

Fortunately, there are standard practices as far as manuscript layout is concerned. You should use good quality 8½ x 11-inch white bond paper. Your manuscript should be printed on one side of each page. Use a standard, easy-to-read typestyle. I use Courier, probably because my first books were written on a manual typewriter, and I am used to seeing manuscripts in that typestyle. You can also use Ariel, Palatino, or Times, if you prefer. Use 11- or 12-point type.

Your manuscript should be double-spaced, with plenty of margin space. Allow one inch on the top, bottom, and sides. The right margin should be ragged. Do not insert an extra line space between paragraphs. Use a tab space to create paragraph indents.

The manuscript should be paginated consecutively from start to finish. Do not paginate each chapter individually. The page numbers should be in a running head at the top of each page. Include your last name, the title of the manuscript, and the page number in the running head.

The title page of your manuscript must include your name and contact details. I place this at the top left-hand side of the title page. I include my name, address, phone number, and e-mail address.

The title of your manuscript should be centered on the page, about one-third down from the top. Write the title in capital letters. Skip a line, and then write "by" in lowercase. Skip another line, and then write the name you want to see listed as author. This might be a pen name, for instance, or you may want to use a special form of your own name. If your legal name is Jonathan Philip Spencer, but you want the cover of the book to list Jonathan P. Spencer as the author, you would write "Jonathan P. Spencer" under the title. Likewise, if Jonathan did not want to use his own name for any reason, he would place his pen name in this position. However, his true, legal name still needs to be placed in the top left-hand-side of the title page.

Below the title and author name skip another line and then list the number of words in the manuscript. You can either list the total number (63,459, for instance), or round it up or down to the nearest five hundred.

Skip another line and then write down the date on which you are posting the package to your publisher. This is important. If the publisher asks you to revise your manuscript for any reason, the date on the title page tells the publisher's staff if they are handling the first or second version of the manuscript.

Print your manuscript out on a laser, or good quality ink jet printer. An extremely high quality dot matrix printer is acceptable, but does not convey as good an impression as a laser-printed manuscript. As you want your manuscript to look as good as possible, consider employing someone to print out your manuscript on a laser printer if you do not have one.

The pages of the manuscript should be kept loose. Do not staple or bind them together.

| Your Manuscript on Disk

Your publisher will also want to have your manuscript on either a Macintosh or Windows disk. Each chapter should be saved separately. The manuscript is unwieldy and difficult to deal with when saved as one file. Each chapter should be saved as "text only." This eliminates production problems later on, as by saving as "text only" you eliminate the formatting codes. However, it is better to print the hard copy of the manuscript using the formatting codes, before saving it as "text only." This enables the editors to see how you envisaged the layout of the book, particularly the headings. I find it beneficial to save my manuscript twice, once fully formatted, and again as text only. This is because I find it easier to deal with editorial queries using the formatted version of the manuscript.

The disk needs to be labeled with your name, title of the manuscript, the software used to create the files, and the date.

| Your Cover Letter

Your cover letter is the first thing that the staff in the Acquisitions Department will see. Its purpose is to introduce you and your manuscript to the publisher. It should be brief, accurate, and to the point. State your qualifications for writing the book, but err on the side of modesty, rather than exaggerating your skills and experience.

Naturally, you should try to sell the book, but avoid phrases such as "This is the best book ever written on this subject." Amazingly, some authors try to sell their books by belittling books that the publisher has already published on the same subject. This is insulting to the publisher, and will lessen your chances of acceptance.

Address your letter to the correct person in the publisher's office. This information can be found in *Literary Marketplace* and *Writer's Market,* and from the publisher's guidelines.

Here is a sample letter:

Nancy J. Mostad,
Acquisitions and Development Manager,
Llewellyn Worldwide Limited,
P.O. Box 64383,
St. Paul, MN 55164-0383

Dear Ms. Mostad,

Enclosed is my manuscript of CRYSTAL BALL DIVINA-TION, which I hope will be suitable for your list. It contains seven proven techniques for seeing images in the crystal ball that my students and I have devised over the last five years. The first half of the book explains how to scry, or crystal gaze, while the second half teaches the reader how to interpret the images. It is a practical, how-to-do-it book that I feel will be popular with your readers.

I have been involved with the psychic world since I was a teenager, and for several years made my living as a crystal ball reader at the Upscale Market near my home. For the last five years I have been teaching classes on how to read the crystal ball. This book is the result of our explorations and discoveries. None of the methods explained have appeared in print before.

I have filled out your Author Questionnaire, and the Biographical Data and Book Information Form, and enclose these with the manuscript, and disk of the mss on Microsoft Word.

I enclose a #10 SASE for your decision. Please recycle the manuscript if it is not suitable for your needs. I look forward to hearing from you soon.

Yours sincerely,

Wood B. Author

This letter is all that is required. It gives the acquisitions department some insight into both the book and the author.

| ADDITIONAL INFORMATION

The publisher's guidelines tell you exactly what they want. Llewellyn Publications insists that all submitted manuscripts include an author questionnaire and an author biographical data and book information form. There is no point in submitting a manuscript to Llewellyn without including these, as the guidelines clearly state that "your submission will not be reviewed without them."

The author questionnaire tells Llewellyn about you and your book. It is your chance to sell you and your manuscript to them. You have spent months working on your manuscript. Do not rush through this stage. Take whatever time is necessary to produce an author questionnaire that sells you and your project to the company. You have 250 words to write about yourself, your strengths, talents, and interests. You also have up to five hundred words to sell your book to the ultimate reader.

The author biographical data and book information form is easier, as all you have to do is fill in the blanks. This form provides Llewellyn with essential information about you. They want to know your legal name, the name you want listed on the title page, your address, contact details, social security number, occupation, birth details, and fluency with foreign languages.

They also want information about the book: the title, subtitle, number of words and pages, details of the computer disk, number of photographs, charts, tables and illustrations. They need to know if you have included a bibliography, glossary, and index. The final questions concern the primary audience for the book, the subject, if it is a translation from a foreign language, and if it has been previously published before in an English-language edition.

All of this information helps Llewellyn assess the book. It is well worth spending extra time on this stage to make sure that you have provided complete, accurate, and helpful answers to all the questions.

| Book Proposals

A book proposal is basically a sales pitch to the publisher. You are attempting to convince the publisher that your idea for a book is a good one, and that you are the perfect person to write it. You are selling both the book idea and yourself. The aim of a book proposal is to receive a positive response from the publisher. Ideally, this would be a contract. More realistically, it will be a letter asking you to finish the book and submit it.

There are advantages and disadvantages to submitting a book proposal, instead of a complete manuscript. You can spend time coming up with fresh ideas, rather than working on the book, if the publishers are not interested in your proposal. This saves you time and energy. The publishers may like your book proposal, but have suggestions as to how you should approach it. This also saves a great deal of time in rewriting and revision later on. Another advantage a proposal has over a completed manuscript is that the publisher assumes the material is fresh, and the manuscript has not already been rejected by other publishers.

What are the disadvantages? It is unlikely that you will be offered a contract until the book has been written. This is especially the case if you have not written previous books for this publisher. You might write the book following the suggestions of the publisher, and still have it rejected. This might mean major rewriting before you can offer it to another publisher.

A book proposal is in three parts. A complete book proposal is included in chapter five. At the very least, a proposal should include a cover letter, an outline of what you intend to include in the book, and one or two sample chapters.

| THE COVER LETTER

This is similar to the cover letter discussed earlier. Every possible way in which you can be contacted should be clearly listed at the top of the page. Include your address, phone numbers (mobile and home), fax numbers and e-mail details. If your book proposal is exactly what the publisher needs, you do not want him or her searching for ways to contact you.

Make sure that you are sending the proposal to the right person and address him or her by name. Start the letter by saying that you are currently writing a book on a topic that you think will interest this publisher. It is possible that you have already finished the book, and are sending in the proposal in the hope of attracting the publisher's interest. If so, do not say that you have already written the book. This is because you may receive a letter back suggesting specific changes that you will need to attend to before sending the manuscript in.

Follow this with a brief description of the book. Two or three sentences are sufficient, as you are including a detailed proposal with the letter.

Tell the publisher what market you are writing the book for. Interested beginners? Professional astrologers? Teenagers? Be as specific as possible. No book is suitable for everyone. If you have your imaginary person in mind, you will be able to come up with a list of the categories of people who would be interested in reading your book.

Include a paragraph that describes you and your expertise in the subject you are writing about. Why are you the perfect person to write this book? Include any relevant qualifications or experience you have that will help sell you as the logical author. Do not include anything that is not relevant. You may have successfully sold vacuum cleaners for fifteen years, but unless this pertains in some way to the topic of your book leave it out. The fact that you studied creative writing or English literature at college is relevant information, though, as it tells the publisher that you might be capable of writing a book. Naturally, mention any publishing credits you may have. They help to establish your credentials as a writer.

Offer to send in any more information or material that the publisher would like to see. Finish the letter by expressing the hope that your submission will be of interest to the publisher, and that you look forward to hearing from him or her.

| Outline

An outline is a one- or two-page summary of your book. In practice, I find it easiest to do this in the form of an annotated table of contents. This says exactly what I intend to include in every chapter.

| Annotated Table of Contents

You will probably have this already, because of the exercises we did earlier. A table of contents lists the chapter headings. An annotated table of contents includes a sentence or two for each chapter to let the publisher know what you will be including. It is not necessary to provide details about the preface, introduction, glossary, notes, bibliography, or index. However, these, and everything else that you will be including in the book need to be listed.

With this information, the publisher will be able to see exactly what the book will contain.

| Sample Chapters

The purpose of the sample chapters is to show the publisher that you can express yourself clearly and well on paper. Consequently, you need ensure that they are as good as possible. Ideally, you should include the Introduction, Chapter One, and one other chapter.

| Putting It Together

Check everything carefully before sending your book proposal package to the publisher. Make sure that the letter is addressed to the right person, and that his or her name is spelled correctly. Find someone who is good at English to read through everything you intend to include. Ideally, this should be someone who is not familiar with the subject of your book. Ask him or her to check for comprehension, spelling, and readability.

Check through everything again, and then send it to your chosen publisher, remembering to include a self-addressed stamped envelope.

| Celebrate and Start the Next Book

The final step is to celebrate. Take the family out for dinner, or do something else that involves the special people in your life. You all deserve it after the amount of time and effort you have put in.

You also need to remain patient. It might be weeks or even months before your submission is examined. If you have sent in a book proposal, rather than the entire manuscript, you can use this waiting time for further research, or you may decide to write another chapter or two. I normally take a day or two off, especially after submitting a complete manuscript, and then start on my next book. Focusing on the new book stops me from thinking about the manuscript I've just posted.

Publishers are extremely busy people and it might take up to six months before you hear back from them. Naturally, you will think about your manuscript from time to time, but the time will pass more quickly if you busy yourself on the next project.

10

Inside the Publisher's Office

You have sent off your manuscript, and are now rushing out to check the mail every day. Naturally, you are anxious, and as the days and weeks go by, you become concerned about the fate of your book. Strangely enough, it is usually good news if it takes a long time to hear back. If the manuscript is totally unsuitable for the publisher, it will come back as soon as it has received a cursory evaluation.

| The Acquisitions Department

When your manuscript arrives at the publisher's office it is delivered to the acquisitions department for its first evaluation. Many submissions get turned down at this stage, frequently because the authors have failed to follow the submission guidelines. The manuscript might not be accompanied with the author questionnaire, for instance. It might be handwritten, or typed entirely in capital letters. The subject matter might be totally unsuitable for the publisher. A book on the joys of keeping hamsters would not be suitable for Llewellyn, for instance, although it might be perfect for another publisher.

If the manuscript passes this first, most basic evaluation, it is put on schedule for an acquisition meeting. At Llewellyn, this meeting comprises the president of the company, the acquisitions manager, and other department managers. All of the author's correspondence, biographical material, and a few sample chapters of the submission are distributed to the committee so they can read it before attending the meeting. At the acquisition meeting, the submission is discussed to determine if the submission's topic and treatment fit Llewellyn's subject matter and audience.

The author's background, as outlined in the biographical questionnaire, is also reviewed, not only for authority and credibility, but also for publicity purposes. This is why it is important for authors to "sell" their own experience when they submit a manuscript. In the New Age field, of course, many authors have no formal academic training, but it is still important that they explain their own studies, experience, community contacts, and previous publications or media exposure.

The acquisition committee also discusses the book's topic and treatment. For example, there are many books on reading the tarot, but one author may focus on using a Jungian approach to interpreting the cards, while another argues for stream-of-consciousness interpretation. The author's tone, too, is evaluated, as appropriate to the topic and the potential audience. These aspects of the submission are considered in and of themselves, but also in terms of the market. Every publisher has to balance what's been successful in the past with what will represent a new and refreshing approach.

Last, but certainly not least, the acquisitions committee looks at the sample chapters. Even given the importance of all the other factors—publicity, marketing, sales—the book is the actual product. The committee wants to see strong writing and organization. If the table of contents and the chapter summary suggest a severe lack of organization or an incomplete presentation, or if the writing is consistently weak, the committee may decide not to expend any more effort on review.

However, if the proposal is interesting and well presented, it advances to the next stage. If needed, a full manuscript or any additional material is requested from the author, then the whole package is sent for an external review. External reviewers are usually freelancers hired by publishers because they have the necessary experience or specialized knowledge of a particular subject. They may also have writing or publishing experience, but in general, their outlook is closer to that of a target book-buyer than a publishing employee. Ideally, an external review gives the publisher a cohesive, detailed report on the submission from the outside. (See the next section for more information on the external review.)

Once the external review is completed and returned, it is taken back to the acquisitions committee meeting. The committee members consider the report and decide on the next step. If the external review strongly criticizes the submission, and backs that up with a detailed explanation, the committee will look into those objections. If they agree, then the submission might be rejected there and then. If the external reviewer provisionally endorses the submission, the committee may act on the reviewer's suggestions. For example, a manuscript may be fascinating and well-written, but is 800 pages long and aimed at a relatively small audience. The reviewer may question whether it can be produced for a viable cover price, and to answer that, the acquisitions department will ask the print buyer and sales manager for more information.

The reviewer may also make suggestions for manuscript alterations: trimming, adding material, reorganizing, resolving permission questions, etc., and the committee may decide to send those suggestions back to the author. These suggestions are usually for more large-scale issues. When this occurs, the publisher is showing interest in the project, but doesn't consider it ready for a final decision. Unless the publisher clearly indicates otherwise, these suggestions do not create any obligation on either side. The author is not obliged to follow the revision suggestions, and the publisher is not obliged to accept any revised manuscript.

If an external review is "on the fence" or is favorable, the acquisitions committee usually votes to send it on to an in-house review. At Llewellyn, this in-house review is done by another committee and is called the vision process. It's hoped that the vision review, with input from several departments, will not only result in a contracting decision, but will also produce a "vision" of what the final product will be. Although it sounds ethereal, the vision process is actually down-to-earth and business oriented. Each committee member is given a complete copy of the submission, and reads it from his or her own perspective. The editor makes notes on editorial issues, the sales department compares data from similar books, the marketing department forms a picture of the target audience and how to reach them, the publicity department suggests which venues and what kind of campaign would best match the author and book, etc.

Once the vision committee decides to either reject a project or offer a contract, they notify the acquisitions manager, who handles the actual correspondence with the author. There are different types of rejection letters, but in every case, an effort is made to be considerate and businesslike.

If a submission was unsolicited, and there's been little contact between the author and publisher during the review process, the author will probably receive a form letter. A common phrase goes something like, "The submission does not fit our needs at this time," which may sound like a bromide but is probably pretty close to the truth. A rejection might not reflect an author's professional failure or a publisher's blindness to genius. More likely it reflects a business reality such as how the publisher's front list is shaping up or what their long-range plans are. Even if the rejection is due to more qualitative issues, the author won't hear it. What one publisher thinks of a project will not reflect what all publishers think, so there's little point in handing out criticism. For those reasons, rejection letters are kept short, direct, and professional.

So much for the bad news. Now, if the publisher decides to offer a contract, the author will receive that fabled "thicker envelope." Inside will be a copy of the company's publishing agreement and a cover letter from the acquisitions manager briefly explaining the next step.

After reviewing the publishing agreement, or having it reviewed by an agent or lawyer, the author is free to negotiate or ask questions. Because the publisher needs to know whether a title should be scheduled for production, put in a particular catalog, opened on the customer service computer for pre-orders, etc., it's best to complete the contracting process as quickly as possible. The author should be careful not to rush into signing the first contract he or she is offered, but dragging the process out unnecessarily is a risk, too.

While contracting is still in progress, Llewellyn sometimes contacts the author about editorial changes. These changes are usually the direct result of the vision meeting, where the project is discussed in more detail. The editor may point out that there is no bibliography or index, or that a glossary would be a useful addition for the intended audience. The art department may request that manuscript illustrations be resubmitted as prints rather than computer files. Or the acquisitions editor will note some quoted material that needs a copyright release. Those requests are gathered together and explained in a letter from the preproduction editor. The author may want to wait, of course, until the contract is signed before doing any additional work, but by bringing up the issues early in the process, Llewellyn feels it is giving the author as much time as possible to fulfill the requests.

If contracting goes well, and any requested changes are clarified and agreed on, the project passes out of the acquisitions department and on to all its other phases. It is worth emphasizing here that those other phases may not begin immediately. Occasionally, new authors will call the acquisitions department after a few weeks asking what's "become of" their project. It feels to the author that the initial flurry of activity around contracting and requested revisions has suddenly dissipated, and been replaced by . . . silence. Those calls are a good reminder for publishers that the length and pace of production schedules are often a surprise to new authors. Once in awhile there will be an unexpected open slot in an upcoming catalog, or a new project will be slated for a special event, and then everything is rushed into production. However, most of the time, a publisher is working a year or more in the future. An author may think, *my book isn't going to be released until when?!* But on the other end, there are editors, graphic designers, publicists, copywriters, and print buyers thinking, *how are we going to get it done that fast?!* So, for a new author, understanding what is involved in every project may ease anxieties.

At Llewellyn, the first step after contracting is transmittal, so-called because the project is transmitted to the production department. The preproduction editor gathers together the manuscript, disk copy, biographical material, and any relevant correspondence. A long form is completed, recapturing the production and editorial details of the vision meeting. Altogether, this is the transmittal package. This is given to the production department assistant, who logs it in and creates an editorial file.

As the assigned editor's overall schedule dictates, a production planning meeting is set up, and here the editor finalizes the details of the project schedule. The editor also reviews the transmittal package to make sure everything is in order, and may discuss illustration or design needs with the art director or design specialist. After this production planning meeting, the editor will contact the author to introduce him- or herself and discuss the project.

Ideally, an author will talk to his or her editor first, since the editor will be the primary contact during production. However, it is possible that the author will hear first from the art department regarding the final book title and cover art. It's easy to think of the cover as the icing on the cake, but it's actually one of the first production steps. The reason for this is that a publisher's catalog goes to print several months in advance; thus, booksellers can plan their orders. Since catalogs usually contain a "thumbprint" illustration of each book's cover, the art department actually finalizes the design of the cover art before editorial work even begins. At Llewellyn, this meeting initiates the part of the process known as launch.

After launch and production planning, the editor will begin production of the book. Various publishers offer various levels of author involvement in editorial decisions, but it is best for everyone if communication is open and healthy. It's often simply not possible to accommodate an author's every request, but editors generally do their best. Editors are book-lovers, and they recognize that a manuscript isn't just a pile of papers. It's the result of the author's hard work in research and writing. In return, a smart author realizes that an editor is working hard, too, to present the book in the best possible light. If there are disagreements during production, they should be handled, from both ends, calmly and professionally.

The imperious author who thinks her or his masterwork is ready to go to the printer "as is" is only a comic cliché for most editors, but the novice author really unsure of how a manuscript becomes a book is a pretty common reality. Editing, typesetting, design, and printing are specialized fields, like many other professions. Now that so many people are familiar with personal computers, word processing, or even desktop publishing, that technology gap may be smaller. Nevertheless, most authors have not undertaken the complete production of a book and may be a bit in the dark.

An editor needs to be familiar with a manuscript before starting work on it. They have to be able to see both the smaller details and the bigger picture. There's an embarrassing typo on page 89, but also, what page layout and design elements are most appropriate to the subject matter? What line lengths and typefaces affect readability? What text elements would be improved with illustrations? Is the chapter organization optimal? Would footnotes benefit readers more than endnotes? In making all these decisions, an editor goes over the entire manuscript carefully and considers the book as a whole. They understand not only the author's position and the readers' needs, but the limitations of design and printing as well. Editing is by far the most detailed and consuming part of book production.

Once the book is edited and typeset, it goes through a round of proofreading, a second edit, and corrections before the author is given a set of page proofs. Proofs show the author what editorial changes have been made and how the book will look in print. At this point, the author can make additional changes and discuss any concerns with the editor, and they should definitely take advantage of this early opportunity. The editor will specify a deadline for the return of the author's corrected proofs, allowing enough time to prepare the final pages and electronic files for the printer. It is extremely important that the author return the proofs on time with all changes they wish made. Changes get costlier and more time-consuming as the process moves along, and eventually making author alterations is no longer feasible. The production schedule is running out, and the book is already scheduled for press time. It's often hard for authors to know when to stop making those final touches to proofs, but the sooner they do, the sooner they'll have their printed book in hand.

Also during the production period, the author may be contacted by the publicity and/or marketing departments to discuss plans for advertising, media opportunities, tours, workshops, websites, and the like. Again, publishers follow various plans for publicizing a new release. Moreover, different subjects and genres are handled in specific ways. For example, it might be decided that a how-to guide on a "hot" topic would benefit greatly from an author tour, while publicity for another more serious book should concentrate on print media and reviews. What the author is available for and willing to do, too, is an important part of publicity, and should be worked out well in advance.

| The External Review

An outside reader is someone who is an expert on the subject of the book. He or she is not necessarily one of the publisher's authors. This person will read the book, and review it for the publisher. This report follows a standard format.

First of all, the title and subtitle of the manuscript, and the author's details are listed. Then the reader answers a series of questions. The first of these is the most important: "Is publication recommended?" Obviously, the answer is either yes or no.

The next question is: "What is the work about? Please give a detailed overview of the subject and how it is presented by the author. If relevant, provide a chapter-by-chapter summary." It can take several pages to answer this question. The reader has to read, absorb, and think about the manuscript before answering.

The next questions are easier to answer. "Does the author write well?" This is an important question. Obviously, there will be less work required in the editorial stages if the book is well written. If the author has written an important book on a certain subject, but does not write well, the editors will have a major job to do if the book is accepted.

"Is the manuscript well organized?" If necessary, the reader will make suggestions on how to improve the organization of the book.

"What is unique and valuable about this book? Why should we publish it?" This is an important question. There is no point in publishing yet another book on the tarot, for instance, unless the manuscript has something different to offer.

"Do you recommend any additional material to enhance the value of the work?" The reader is already knowledgeable about the subject of the book. Having read this manuscript, he or she is in a good position to suggest ideas that could increase the value of the book.

"Will the manuscript require expert editing? Extensive copy editing?" Ideally, the answer to this is no. Every book needs editing, but if the amount of editing required drives production costs too high the project cannot be profitable, and the publisher will either decide not to publish the book, or will ask the author to do a major rewrite.

"Please list any suggestions or concerns (e.g., factual errors, inconsistencies, clarity problems) directed to the author's or editor's attention, giving page references." The reader frequently makes suggestions that will enhance the book. He or she is looking at the manuscript in a detached manner, and can often see things that the author has overlooked. The reader's concerns can also be helpful. In one of my books, I mentioned something about the Oracle of Delphi that was incorrect. I had checked the information in what I thought was a reputable book, but this source was wrong. If the reader had not picked this up, I would have inadvertently passed on that incorrect information to my readers.

The next section of the report covers the specifications of the manuscript. The publisher needs to know how the manuscript is submitted, the size of the work, and whether it contains a glossary, index, bibliography, or illustrations. The reader is asked to point out any production concerns he or she has. These could include unusual or special type fonts, artwork that would be expensive or complicated to reproduce, etc.

The final part of this section is for the reader to point out any obvious permission problems. The author may have included lengthy quotations from other books, or included artwork or charts from other published works. Naturally, any issues that could be libelous or invade someone's privacy need to be included here, as well as any advice or instructions that might be potentially dangerous.

The next section is on the book's marketability. The reader is asked to provide an alternative title, and/or subtitle, if it is felt necessary.

"Does the work fit the Llewellyn model of practical how-to and self-help (application of technology)? A practical reference work? A new development of theoretical foundation knowledge? The *FATE* model of 'True Stories of the Strange and Unknown'? Or does it establish a new direction for Llewellyn?" Ideally, the manuscript will fit comfortably into the Llewellyn guidelines. If it does not, the chances of it being accepted are limited.

"To what market is the work directed?" The author will have given his or her answer to this question in the author questionnaire. The reader may suggest other markets that the author has not considered.

"Suggested price range." The answer to this is important. If the manuscript is 300,000 words long and the suggested price range is between eight and ten dollars, the publisher would have to approve a large print run to be able to sell it at this price. If the book is aimed at a limited market, the publisher might have to reject the book on cost grounds.

"What is the competition like? How does this product differ? How can it be made to stand above similar titles?" The author should have provided this information in the author's questionnaire. The reader will have his or her opinion, which may differ to that of the author.

"Do any spin-off ideas come to mind?" The reader has an opportunity to put forward ideas that will help sales of the book. He or she might suggest marketing the book with a deck of cards, or perhaps producing it in a different form, such as on CD.

The final section of the reader's report is concerned with the author.

"Do we have a photo? Do we have guideline responses?" If this is your first book with Llewellyn, they will not have a photograph, but guideline responses should have been included with the submission.

"What about the author's background, qualifications, or experience do you think can best be promoted?" The author will have provided information about him- or herself with the submission. Based on this, the reader will make suggestions to help promote the book.

"Do you have any particular concerns about the author?" Hopefully, the answer will be "no," but this question gives the reader an opportunity to express any doubts he might have.

"Even if we reject this submission, is this an author who might be encouraged in another area or for another product? Any suggestions for such?" It is never pleasant to be rejected, but the answers to these questions can provide helpful advice for the author. The reader might suggest a topic that had not occurred to the author, for instance.

As you can see, the reader's report provides Llewellyn with a large amount of information. Based on this, the manuscript can proceed to the next stage.

| REJECTION

No one likes to be rejected, and it can be a devastating moment when you hear that the manuscript you labored over for so long has been turned down. The first thing to remember is that you are not being rejected. The publisher is rejecting your manuscript, not you. You might like to read *Pushcart's Complete Rotten Reviews and Rejections.*[1] This book contains rejection letters sent to people who later became famous in their fields. Eric Ambler, John Barth, Pearl Buck, Julia Child, William Faulkner, Ernest Hemingway, Stephen King, John Le Carré, Dr. Seuss, and H. G. Wells are among the examples.

Allow at least a few days to pass before doing anything further with your manuscript. It is natural to think about your book and the rejection letter during this time, but try not to dwell on it. Hopefully, you will already be well into your next book, and working at this will help take your mind off the rejection.

If you receive a copy of the reader's report with your manuscript, you will be able to see what he or she felt was wrong with your submission. You may disagree with the assessment. In that case, send your manuscript to another publisher. If you are convinced that your manuscript needs no improvement, keep on submitting it until you receive an acceptance. *Jonathan Livingston Seagull* received twenty rejections before being accepted.[2] It is more likely, though, that the reader made specific comments about the book, and you should read your manuscript again, with the reader's concerns in mind.

Many problems can be rectified, but first you have to find out exactly what they are. If you are unable to determine these yourself, ask someone who is familiar with the subject of your book to read it. Explain that it has been rejected by a publishing house and that you know there is something wrong with it. Ask for the truth. Your close friends and family are likely to tell you how wonderful the book is, because they love you and do not want to upset you. This is why it is better to find someone who will be able to read the book and give you an objective viewpoint.

Maybe the book was not suitable for the publisher, even though you thought it was. A friend of mine wrote a humorous book on divination that he thought Llewellyn would publish. They turned it down, but it was immediately taken up by a humor book publisher. He had written a good book, but had sent it to the wrong publisher. Make sure that your topic is one that is covered in the publisher's guidelines.

Check your approach to the subject, and compare it with the approach other authors have made to the same subject. It is possible that your book might be overly academic, for instance. That is perfect if you are looking for an academic publisher, but is not the best approach for a more general publisher.

Perhaps the book was rejected because your writing was not good enough. In that case, take adult education classes to develop your writing skills. Maybe you neglected to revise the book before sending it to a publisher. Erle Stanley Gardner's 90 percent rejection rate when he first started writing was because he did not revise his work before sending it out.

Check your cover letter and author questionnaire. Did you provide the required information adequately, honestly, and completely? In the case of a book proposal, did you do a good job with your outline and sample chapters? These things need to be checked and corrected, if necessary, before sending the manuscript to another publisher.

Sad to say, luck can play a part, as well. The publisher may have recently accepted a manuscript from another author on the same subject. In this instance, the publisher may have to reluctantly turn down a perfectly good manuscript, rather than bring out two books on the same subject at the same time. A small publisher may have accepted all the titles he can afford to publish this year. Consequently, he is forced to reject everything that arrives once his list is full.

Finally, you need to decide if you are prepared to thoroughly revise your manuscript to make it suitable for publication. Even if you discard it, the work you put into it will not be wasted. The more writing you do, the better you become. Most professional writers have a number of unpublished manuscripts hidden away somewhere. Writing these gave them the skills to ultimately become successful authors. You might feel it better to put this manuscript away, at least for a while, and start on a new book, using the skills that you developed while writing the first one.

| PUBLICATION AT ANY COST

If you are determined to get your book published, no matter what, there are a number of other alternatives that you could look at. For many years I worked as a ghost writer, writing books for other people.

Some ghost writers work as "book doctors." They help authors to rewrite and rearrange their books to make them more suitable for publication. This is an expensive option, with no guarantee of publication at the end of it. However, if you find a good ghost writer, you will learn many useful skills that you will be able to use in later books.

The best way to find a ghost writer is by word of mouth. Alternatively, magazines such as *Writer's Digest* contain advertisements from ghost writers. Before employing one, speak to two or three of their former clients. You want to employ a ghost writer with a successful track record, so it is important to choose one who has happy clients. You also want to make sure that the ghost writer you employ is going to work on your manuscript him- or herself. Some book doctors employ students and assign this sort of work to them.

Another alternative is to find a co-author. When you employ a ghost writer, his or her name does not appear on the published book; a co-author's name does. You would be looking for an arrangement where you provide expert knowledge of the subject, and your co-author provides the necessary writing skills. It is important that you choose this person carefully. As you will be working together for a long time, you need someone you will be able to get along with. A co-author will share the royalties with you.

| SUBSIDY PUBLISHING

You might be tempted by the advertisements of vanity publishers. These are publishers who advertise in magazines seeking authors. These people call themselves "subsidy" publishers, because the idea is that you subsidize the costs of publication. In fact, you pay a large sum of money for all the costs of publication. I have met several authors who were published by subsidy publishers. All of them paid dearly for the experience. The problem is that most subsidy houses provide little in the way of editorial services. Consequently, the faults that prevented the book from being published by a normal publisher are still present in the finished book. Book reviewers and bookstores also tend to ignore books published by subsidy publishers. Although these publishers offer a high royalty (as much as 40 percent), this is irrelevant if few books are being sold.

| SELF-PUBLICATION

Self-publication is another alternative. It is comparatively simple to produce your own book these days, but this route is also full of pitfalls. When you self-publish, you take on all the costs and risks of publication. You need to be a good business person to make a success of this. I know a number of people with garages full of unsold books.

Self-publish only if you are certain that you will be able to sell the books you produce. Perhaps you speak in public regularly, and are able to sell books after your talks. Maybe you can sell copies through organizations you belong to. Even then, print as few copies as you can. Test carefully before investing large sums of money in your book.

The biggest fault I find with self-published books is that they advertise the fact that they are self-published. Employ a professional editor to edit the book for you. It is not possible to do this yourself. I have worked as an editor, but would not dream of editing my own work. Employ a professional designer to lay out the book for you. Choose a graphic artist who has had experience at designing book covers. All of this is expensive, which is why you have to be certain that you will sell enough copies to recoup your costs.

Yet another possibility is to publish your work as an e-book. You can either do this yourself, or use one of the many e-book publishers who will put your book on the web for a monthly fee. This may sound like a cheap option, but even here, your book should be professionally edited before placing it on the worldwide web. Once it is up there, you will have to promote it continually, as nobody will buy it unless they know of its existence. The competition is increasing on the web all the time, and you will need to promote your book constantly. One of the best ways to do this is to post replies to comments made on news groups that relate to the subject of your book. If you have your website listed under your name, many people who read your comments will decide to check out your site.

There are two main problems with publishing your manuscript as an e-book. The first is that many authors with unsold manuscripts are publishing them themselves. Unfortunately, most of these books are extremely bad. If someone buys one of these, he or she is most unlikely to ever buy another. The other problem is that most people expect to find what they want on the Internet free of charge. There is a disinclination to pay for anything, as well as fears about the security of sending credit card information over the Internet. This makes it hard, but not impossible, to make money out of all the time and effort that is involved. You need to be a good marketer to be successful at any form of self-publishing.

11
CONTRACTS

For a writer, next to receiving your first copy of the published book, there can be few feelings better than receiving a publisher's contract in the mail. Your book has been accepted, and you are on your way to becoming a published author.

However, after the first moments of euphoria, you have to read your contract. You might find that deciphering the legal language in which your contract is written leaves you more confused than ever. It is important that you understand every detail of your contract. If necessary, ask a lawyer to explain it to you. Most publishing contracts are fairly standard, though they vary in length and in the way different sections are phrased.

You might decide that this is a good time to find an agent. A good agent will help you negotiate the contract, and is likely to negotiate better terms than you could yourself. However, you will have to decide if it is worth giving up a percentage of your royalties. This is especially the case if your book is aimed at a limited audience, which naturally reduces your potential royalties anyway.

A contract attorney or an intellectual property attorney will negotiate a contract for a fee, rather than a percentage of the book's proceeds. They are involved with the contract, but then have no further interest in the book. As publishing contracts are usually different to contracts in other fields, it is important that you employ a professional who has had experience with book contracts and the publishing industry.

If you decide to employ someone to help you, make sure that you select that person carefully. You will be working with this person for as long as the contract remains valid, so it is important that you feel that you will get on well together.

I do not use an agent, and have not found this to be a hindrance in my career. When I first started as a writer, I could not find an agent who would take me on. Now that I am established, agents approach me. If you want an agent, the perfect time to approach one is when you have a contract to sign. This represents guaranteed income for the agent, and you will receive a better reception than you would if trying to find an agent with an unaccepted manuscript.

There are two excellent books on book contracts that you should study while you go through your book contract. They are: *The Writer's Legal Companion* by Brad Bunnin and Peter Beren,[1] and *Negotiating a Book Contract: A Guide for Authors, Agents, and Lawyers* by Mark L. Levine.[2]

Read through your contract several times to make sure that you understand it. This can prevent problems and misunderstandings later. One author I know created an e-book of his book and offered it for sale over the Internet. He did this innocently, assuming that he owned the Internet rights of his work. However, his contract with the publisher said otherwise, and he had to take his e-book off the market. The exercise cost him a great deal of time and expense, and jeopardized his future relationship with the publisher. If he had read through his contract carefully in the first place, none of that would have happened.

A publishing contract begins by identifying you ("hereinafter referred to as the 'Author,'") the publisher ("hereinafter referred to as the 'Publisher'"), and the tentative title of your manuscript (which is called the "Work").

It then goes on to describe the rights that you are giving to the publisher, and the royalties you will receive as a result. The rights you give to the publisher include the exclusive rights to allow third parties to "publish, transmit and/or sell distinct editions of said Work" in a variety of forms, which may include film, television, CD-ROM, and e-book editions. These are known as subsidiary rights. The royalties the publisher receives from these additional sales is shared with you, as the author.

The publisher agrees to copyright the work in the United States in your name. This means that the work is copyrighted until fifty years after your death. [Ed. Note: The U.S. Congress recently upheld 1998 legislation that extended copyrights to seventy years.]

All rights to your book revert back to you if the publisher allows the book to go out of print for more than one year. However, you have to advise the publisher in writing of your intent to take the rights back. The publisher then has up to 120 days to announce that he will be producing a new edition.

The contract will stipulate what the publisher requires from you regarding the completed manuscript, and any extra materials, such as charts, diagrams, and photographs. It will also stipulate that you need to obtain written permission from the copyright holders of any extracts you intend including in your book. The usual contract allows you 180 days to do whatever is necessary to bring your work up to publication standard.

Naturally, the payment of your royalties is important. The Llewellyn contract states that you will receive an accounting of all monies received by the publisher on or before September 30 and March 31 each year. In September you will receive an accounting of all sales made and paid for during the first half of the calendar year. In March you learn about the sales in the second half of the preceding year. Payment of the royalties are made thirty days after each accounting.

As part of the contract, you will be asked to submit your next book-length work in your publisher's areas of interest to the publisher, before offering it to anyone else.

| Negotiation

Everything in a contract can be negotiated. However, reputable publishers will offer you a fair contract, and there are unlikely to be many areas that you would need to negotiate. A contract is naturally weighted in the publisher's favor, but the publisher will want to have a long-term, mutually beneficial relationship with you. The publisher will want to publish your future books as well, and will not jeopardize that by offering you an unfair contract.

All the same, there may be areas that you wish to negotiate. For instance, if you make a large part of your living as a speaker or trainer, you might want to negotiate a larger discount for copies you buy yourself, so that you can sell them to attendees at your classes or workshops. This would only be worth doing if you were buying hundreds of books at a time. If you were doing only occasional seminars, it would be better to ask a local bookstore to provide books to sell. You would not make any immediate money, but would create enormous goodwill with the bookstore, who would be more likely to actively promote and display your books in the future.

It is vital that you understand every clause of the contract before signing it. Ask the publisher for clarification of anything you do not understand. Once you understand the contract, and agree to it, sign it and return it to your publisher.

| Taxes

It seems fitting to mention taxes while discussing contracts. Authors are self-employed business people who have to pay their own tax bills. You are legally allowed to deduct any legitimate expenses you incur while researching and writing your book. Phone calls, supplies, mileage, and other legitimate expenses can all be deducted. Office furniture can also be claimed. Keep receipts for everything.

You can also claim expenses for a home office, if that room is used primarily for your writing. Unfortunately, you cannot claim this if you do your writing at the kitchen table or in a corner of your living room. The deduction for your home office also includes a percentage of your mortgage or rent payments, property taxes, insurance, utilities, and repairs and maintenance. If your home office takes up 10 percent of the space in your house, you can deduct 10 percent of these costs.

Naturally, you need to find out exactly what you can and can't do from a good accountant. The expertise of my accountant saves me more than his fee every year. Certainly, you can do it yourself, but your time is better spent writing New Age books, rather than working on account books.

12

WORKING WITH EDITORS

Editors play a vital role in ensuring that your book is as perfect and as free of errors as possible when it is presented to the marketplace. It is a difficult task, as they have to remain constantly aware of the needs of the ultimate reader, while simultaneously working for you and the company who pays their wages. Some books need a relatively light edit. This occurs when the author writes well, knows his or her subject, and submits a well-organized, accurate manuscript. This is what you should aim to provide every time you submit a book to a publisher. Other books need heavier editing. One extreme example that I was involved in recently concerned a book written by someone who was not fluent in English. The quality of the material was excellent, but almost every sentence had to rewritten to make it clear for the people who bought the book. A friend of mine is an extremely good technical writer, but he has major difficulties in writing for a general audience. His books always need a great deal of editing to improve their clarity.

Authors of mainstream books constantly worry about their editors. Their biggest concern is that the editor who signed their book will remain with the company at least until the book is published. This is not a problem with New Age publishers. In my experience, the editors in these houses love both editing and the New Age. Consequently, they usually stay with the same publisher for years, enabling you to work with them on many different projects. It is important to have a good working relationship with your editor, and frequently you will become friends.

Every book needs editing, and your editor will work with you to create the very best book possible. Some authors consider editors to be their enemies, but the reality is that they are there to help you. The constructive ideas and suggestions I have received from editors over the years have helped me enormously. Consequently, I am happy that my publisher, Llewellyn, prints the name of the book's editor inside every book. It seems strange to me that most publishers fail to do this, as the editor invariably makes an important contribution to every book he or she works on, and this input should be recognized.

I have worked as an editor, so have had experience dealing with both authors and editors. Although I could probably still edit someone else's book, I would never try to edit my own work. This is why I always encourage self-published authors to employ someone to edit their books before spending large sums of money printing them. No matter how good a writer you are, your writing will benefit enormously from the input of a conscientious editor.

A good editor will make sure that your voice, your own distinctive way of explaining things, remains intact and consistent. This allows your personality to come across, and by the end of the book, the reader will feel that he or she knows you. The reader wants to trust you, and your editor can make that happen by ensuring that you say exactly what you want to say, and do so in a clear and logical manner. Your editor will want your book to be well structured, logical, and well organized. It is a pleasure to read a book of this sort, as the reader subliminally knows that the author is an expert on the subject and will explain everything in a way that the reader will understand.

The first thing authors discover with their first books is that the publishing process is a lengthy one. It can take up to two years for your book to appear in bookstores. You sign the contract, and then hear nothing for what seems like ages. This is because your book will be slotted in to the production process so that it appears in the market at a certain time.

This gives the artist time to create the best-possible book cover for you. The back cover and inside copy is written, catalogs are produced that help promote your book, the sales reps and distributors hear about your book, and many other tasks are undertaken. It all takes time.

You will probably find out who your editor is shortly after your book has been accepted. Remember that he or she will be working on other books as well as yours, so you will need to be patient and wait your turn. Naturally, your editor will be able to answer your queries and concerns more easily once he or she is working on your book. The best thing you can do while waiting is to work on your next book.

... my editor reminds me that she is my partner, not my critic ...

You may feel that your polished prose is perfect as it is, and feel insulted when your editor suggests changes. Understand that you both have the same aims. You both want to produce a book that you will be proud to be associated with. Naturally, you don't have to automatically agree with everything your editor suggests. However, it is worth remembering that your editor is able to look at your book more objectively than you can. Neither will your editor want to make changes just for the sake of it. Consequently, think about the suggested alterations for a day or two before responding. If you still feel strongly about something after this breathing space, contact your editor and explain why you are unhappy with the proposed changes.

Your editor has a major role in the production process. He or she will check every part of your manuscript for accuracy. He or she will ask you to clarify ambiguous passages, and possibly rearrange material to help the overall flow of the book. Grammar and syntax will be checked and corrected.

The book will also have to fit in with the publisher's rules of style. Most publishers use *The Chicago Manual of Style*, published by the University of Chicago Press, but also have house rules of their own. The publisher's house style includes simple matters, such as spelling and punctuation, but also includes how they handle footnotes, quotations, abbreviations, charts, tables, graphs, and type styles.

Your editor might ask you to write more material, if your manuscript is shorter than expected. Likewise, you might be asked to reduce the size of the manuscript if it is too long. Both of these situations create a great deal of extra work. It is better to avoid the necessity for this by providing a manuscript of the correct length in the first place.

Spelling is a major problem for many authors. There is no excuse for this today, as most computers have spell-check programs. However, some authors have the attitude that it is their editor's job to correct any spelling mistakes, and that they need not worry. This is not the case, because anything you can do to make your editor's job easier gives him or her extra time to work on other areas of your book.

| QUERIES

Your editor is likely to have a number of questions that arise while he or she is working on your book. Often, these will arrive with the proofs of your book. However, it is possible that your editor will send you a number of queries while he or she is working on the manuscript. This is especially the case if the questions relate to a large part of the book. Nowadays, most queries come by phone, fax, or e-mail, as the sooner they are addressed, the sooner the editor can return to the book.

Your editor is likely to correct basic grammatical errors without consulting you. Other changes to make the book conform to the publisher's house style will also be made. However, your editor will certainly query any factual inconsistencies, and incomplete or missing footnotes and source notes. Anything that might confuse the reader will be queried, too. Respond to any queries as quickly as possible, to ensure the editing stage is completed on time.

| Proofs

Once the editor has finished working on your book, you will receive a set of proofs. These show you what each page will look like in the finished book. The editor will go through the proofs before sending them to you, and will mark anything that needs clarification or amendment. You need to read the proofs carefully, answer your editor's queries, and let him or her know of any other errors that you find. Typically, you will have up to thirty days to check the proofs and send them back, but I try to get my proofs back within a week. This is because the book has to go to the printer by a certain date, so that it can be published on time, and I want to provide my publishers with all the extra time they may need to prepare it for publication.

This is not an opportunity to rewrite major portions of your book. It is too late, and too expensive, to do any rewriting at this stage. Many publishing contracts stipulate that any major changes be done at the author's expense. Usually, the author is reponsible for the cost of any changes made that exceed 10 percent of the typesetting costs. Llewellyn's contract says: "Any changes in the proofs not in confor-mance with the manuscript as revised prior to typesetting or record-ing will be made only if acceptable to both Author and Publisher, with the cost of such changes as proposed by the Author to be deducted from subsequent royalties due the Author."

Once you return the proofs, your editor will go through them and incorporate any changes and corrections on his or her copy, before sending your book to the printers. He or she might contact you again with a minor query or two, but the next major event is when you re-ceive the first copy of your book in the mail.

If your book is published by Llewellyn, you will receive two copies initially. One is to show to your friends and family. Take time out to celebrate, and show your book to everyone. You have achieved something that most people only dream of accomplishing. Make the most of this exciting time.

The other copy is for you to read carefully to see if you can find any errors that can be corrected in the second printing. Hopefully, you will not find anything, but it is not uncommon for a typo or other minor error to slip through the editing and reading process. Let your editor know about any errors that you find.

It might seem that you have now done everything necessary to ensure the success of your book. In fact, you are only beginning. More than 60,000 new books are published every year in the United States. Your book is just one of them. You need to become actively involved in publicizing and promoting your book. That is the subject of the next chapter.

13

Promoting Your Book

Publicity sells books. The right publicity can sell a lot of books. There are a large number of people who would benefit by reading your book. However, if they do not know it is available, they will not buy it. Publicity brings people into the bookstores to buy your book.

You should start thinking well before the book is published about what you can do to help your book's sales. Many authors dislike publicizing and promoting their books. They feel that their job is to write the books, and it is up to the publisher to sell them. This is correct to a certain extent, and it all depends on how successful you want to be. Your publisher can do only so much, and if you want your book to sell well you need to actively participate. In fact, most of the time, you are the best person to promote your book.

Your publisher will have a publicity and promotion department. Well before the publication release date these people will be coming up with ideas to promote your book. You will be assigned a publicist, who will work with you to capitalize on as many promotional activities as possible. However, your publicist will be working with many other authors at the same time. Consequently, he or she may have limited time to work on your book.

Naturally, some books are easier to promote than others. A book on the history of the Golden Dawn will appeal to a small and enthusiastic group of readers, but it might be hard to interest a talk-show host in the subject. When *Feng Shui for Beginners* came out, the subject was still new and exciting to most people. Consequently, my publicist was able to book me on numerous radio and television programs. It would be harder to do that today, as there are now hundreds of books in print on the subject, and it is not as hot as it was. That is not to say that it cannot be done. It can, and your publicist will be doing everything possible to get your book known in the marketplace.

Your publicist will want to know what you are prepared to do as far as publicity is concerned. Some authors are not willing to do a radio interview, even from their own homes. Consequently, a publicist would probably pass them by and spend more time working with authors who enjoy promoting their wares.

My personal rule is to do anything at all that might help sales. Consequently, I sometimes get up in the middle of the night to talk for a few minutes with a breakfast DJ in the States who cares nothing about my book, but wants someone he can banter with for a few minutes to entertain his audience. New Age books are an easy target for skeptics, and I never know if these brief talks will be positive or negative. However, I don't care what the DJs might say, just as long as the title of the book and my name go out over the air. I usually get back to bed and think of all the smart and witty comments I could have made, but this seldom prevents me from going back to sleep, happy because I've done something that might help the sales of my book.

New Age authors are usually in a better position to promote their books than other types of authors. Many authors of New Age books conduct classes or teach workshops. Consequently, they are used to standing up in front of an audience and speaking. Normally, they can demonstrate or show something to illustrate the talk, and this helps, too.

| DECIDE WHAT YOU ARE PREPARED TO DO

Evaluate yourself carefully, and realistically decide what activities you would be prepared to do to promote your book. Are you willing to go into bookstores to talk about your book and do signings? What about seminars and workshops? Are you happy to go into a radio station and be interviewed by someone who may be skeptical, or even hostile? I have had two experiences with hostile interviewers, once on the radio and again on television. In both cases, the situation worked to my advantage and sold books, but they were stressful at the time. How do you feel about appearing on television?

There is a simple test you can do to determine your willingness to do any promotional activity. Close your eyes, take a few deep breaths, and then think about the proposed activity. Let's imagine that it is a local television show. In your mind's eye; see yourself in the studio. Visualize the person who will be interviewing you, and see yourself answering the first question. Become aware of yourself, and see what response your body is giving to the interview. Is it relaxed? Tense? Slightly stressed? Panicked?

... you are the best person to promote your book ...

If the prospect is terrifying, it might be better to concentrate on other forms of publicity, at least until you gain some confidence. Fortunately, there is a similar test you can do to help become more relaxed and sure of yourself.

Close your eyes and take three deep breaths. Visualize yourself in the television studio in the seconds before the interview starts. Allow the feelings of panic and fear to build up inside you. See this picture becoming smaller and fainter in your mind. Superimpose over it a new scenario. You are in the television studio again, but this time you are relaxed, confident, and in total control. You feel slightly nervous, but this is a good sign, as it means you will perform well. See yourself conducting the interview effectively, answering the questions with a touch of humor, and enjoying the experience. See yourself afterward, happy because the interview went so well. Repeat this exercise as often as possible, until the first scenario is hard to visualize any more.

Even if you are not prepared to be interviewed on the radio, there are still things you can do to publicize and promote your book. You can have business cards printed that show the cover of your book on them. Full-color business cards are not expensive, and you can give these away everywhere you go. You could put a message on your answering machine. After asking people to leave a message, you could add that your new book is now available at all good bookstores. Everything helps.

| Book Signings

The key to a successful book signing is to make it an event. You want it to be memorable for the book store, hopefully because of the large numbers of books they sell, and also for the crowds of people who come in to meet you. This takes forethought and planning.

Last year I went to see and hear a well-known mystery writer who came to my town as part of a book tour to promote his latest book. I wanted to hear what he had to say, and intended to buy his new book. There were about forty people in the store waiting for him. The store manager gave him a wonderful introduction, and then the great man stood up. He said: "I like to write my books," and then sat down again. I was disappointed, particularly as I had given up an evening to hear him and had made a special trip into the city. I left without buying his latest book, and have not read any of his books since.

A striking contrast to this was Lemony Snicket, a hugely successful author of books for ten- to fourteen-year-olds. I had not read any of his books, but went to see his book signing out of curiosity, and because it was at a bookstore only a couple of miles from home.

Lemony was introduced, and entertained a huge crowd of children for almost an hour with an hilarious story of a picnic he had been on that day. His presentation was superb, and his audience—children and adults alike—were captivated. He finished by playing the piano accordion and singing a song, with the help of his audience.

Lemony was in the store to promote his books, and his presentation ensured that almost everyone present bought at least one. Some people lined up with half a dozen books for him to sign. Lemony spoke for almost an hour, and then signed books for at least that amount of time again.

Attend as many author events as you can. No matter what the subject of the book, you will learn from every author. Some, like Lemony Snicket, will be superb. Others will be awful. After each one, think what you would have done if you had been the author, to help sell more books.

Book signings in the traditional sense are usually ineffective. The author is placed behind a table containing a stack of his books, and hopes that people in the store will stop, talk to him, and buy a book. Signings of this sort sometimes work, especially if the author is a celebrity or appeared on television the night before, but usually they are a disappointment.

Your book signing needs to be entertaining and informative. You might be able to give a demonstration of something in your book. You might give an introductory talk on the subject. Whatever you do needs to be interesting enough to encourage people to stop browsing around the book shelves and listen to you.

Tell personal stories. Reveal a little bit about yourself. Relax and have fun. People always want to know how you became interested in the subject. Tell them, preferably in a light-hearted or humorous manner. If possible, have a prop or two, to give people something to look at while you are talking. A handout is a good idea, as it provides something useful for people to take away with them that also just happens to include information about your book.

Be prepared to stay in the store for a while after your talk. If people are interested in what you have to say, they will want to talk to you afterward. Make sure that you attend to the people who want to buy books first, as you will meet many people who want to take up your time but have no intention of buying a book.

In a perfect world the bookstore would do all the advertising and promotion, so that all you need to do is turn up and give a talk, followed by a book signing. The reality is often different. The people who work in bookstores are busy, and often run out of time and sometimes forget about upcoming events. On two occasions I have arrived at a bookstore to give a talk and book signing to find they had no copies of my books in stock. I have also turned up to give a talk and book signing to discover that the store had forgotten about it, and had done no promotion or advertising.

Sometimes the bookstores do nothing whatsoever to promote the event, and simply rely on the universe to bring people in. In my experience, this method never works. Llewellyn provides bookstores with flyers to help promote the event. These are extremely effective when distributed, but sometimes I have arrived at a store to find the flyers sitting on the counter. They are worthless if no one gets to see them.

Consequently, whenever possible, you must help the bookstore promote your event. Mention the upcoming signing on every radio or TV interview. Do a mailing to everyone you know within a reasonable distance of the bookstore. Promote the event on your web page. You cannot do too much to help the bookstore promote the event.

Even if the signing is not a huge success, you will still benefit from the appearance. The staff in the bookstore will get to know you, and will be able to talk about you to their customers. The store will buy an additional stock of your book for the event and will have had a display of them for a week or so before you arrived.

Offer to sign any unsold stock before you leave. People love buying autographed books. Also, the bookstore is much less likely to return autographed books for credit after the promotion is over. Some bookstores have a special table for autographed books, and these sell well as many people will buy a personalized copy of a book in preference to an unsigned copy off the shelves.

Remember to write to the store as soon as possible after the event to thank them for having you.

| RADIO AND TELEVISION

Almost every author I have ever spoken to has expressed a desire to appear on *Oprah*. The chances are that this will not happen, but fortunately there are thousands of smaller radio and television shows that welcome interesting guests. Radio, in particular, is an excellent way to promote your book. You normally have more time to talk on a radio interview than you do on television. The other advantage is that many of these interviews can be done from the comfort of your own home.

Be prepared. It pays to read your book the night before an interview. You possibly wrote the book a few years earlier, and may not remember everything in it. It doesn't hurt to refresh your mind before an interview.

Prepare a list of questions that you have good answers for, and send them to the interviewer in advance. Usually, the interviewer will have his or her own questions to ask, but sometimes, especially on radio, they will be pleased to have the work done for them. Make sure that you have the answers to these questions memorized. Your replies should be insightful, succinct, and helpful. A bit of humor works well, too.

If possible, watch or listen to the program a day or two before your appearance. This will give you a sense of what your interview will be like. The more you know about the program ahead of time, the better.

Do not refer to your book all the time. Naturally, the main reason you are on the show is to promote your book, but it doesn't look good if you are constantly mentioning it. Usually, the host of the show will mention the book for you. This problem will not arise if you ask the host when the book will be mentioned before your segment starts.

A few years ago, an author listened to a radio show the day before her appearance on it. She heard the DJ talk about the crazy woman he was going to have on the following day, and how she actually believed the crazy things she had written about in her book. This author was so terrified at hearing this that she cancelled the interview. The only reason I heard about it was because I was invited on in her place. Naturally, I agreed. The interviewer was extremely skeptical, but mentioned my book several times and gave me sufficient time to rebut his negative comments. I'm sure the interview sold books.

Make sure that you arrive at the radio or television station early. You want to be as relaxed as possible when you are on the air. A few months ago, I had fifteen minutes on *Good Morning Arizona* because the other featured guest was stuck in morning traffic and failed to arrive. I had originally been given five minutes, and the extra time made a huge difference to the bookstore events I had over the following two days.

| Dealing With Your Fans

Writing a book will not change anything as far as your family is concerned. However, from the general public's point of view you have changed for ever. You will become a star to people who have read and enjoyed your work. It is important that you treat your fans with respect. Sometimes they will say or do strange things out of awkwardness. Recently, someone told me she "quite liked" my book. That sounded damning to me, but it was intended as a compliment.

Some years ago, my daughter was working at the leading hotel in our city and noticed a man walking impatiently up and down in the lobby. She went over and asked him if she could help him in any way. He was astonishingly rude to her, one of only two people she found obnoxious in the five years she worked there. She asked a colleague who he was. He was a popular leading author from Britain who was in the country on a book tour. Whoever had been sent to pick him up was late, and he turned his fury and frustration on to my daughter. Until that time, I had been a great fan of this author's books, but I have not bought or read any of his books since. His rudeness to someone who only wanted to help him cost him a loyal fan.

You must keep your feet firmly on the ground. You may have written the best book ever written on the magical arts, which makes you an important person in some people's minds, but that is no reason to put on airs and graces. Be kind, gentle, and generous with your readers when you meet them.

The same thing applies when you meet people who do not like your work and think you are an agent of the devil. Be pleasant, talk with them, and agree to differ. There is nothing to be gained by arguing with them. They will enjoy the argument, and you will lose time and energy.

Remember, also, that skeptics can help you sell books. Almost twenty years ago, I was reading palms in a shopping mall to promote *The Stars and Your Destiny*, one of my early books. The congregation of a local fundamentalist church held hands and encircled the shopping mall. Whenever people wanted to come in, they had to pass through a cordon of people. They were all told about the evil person inside who wanted to read their palms. This protest on their part got me on national television, and I enjoyed the busiest week I ever had in a shopping mall. These people who thought they were doing God's work shouted abuse at me every day when I arrived and left, but I remained pleasant and courteous with them.

You will start receiving fan mail, also. This is flattering and wonderful at first, but it can become incredibly time-consuming and expensive to reply to all of them. I live in New Zealand, which means that every time I buy a stamp to reply to an overseas letter it costs me more than the royalty I received from the sale of the book. Consequently, you can imagine how thrilled I am to receive letters telling me they borrowed the book from their local library. However, I always reply—eventually—to letters.

Sadly, I am no longer able to reply to all the e-mails I receive. I used to answer all of them, even the people who sent me two or three emails a day for weeks on end. However, I now receive well over a hundred e-mails a day, and would have no time to write my books if I replied to them all. So, reluctantly, I had to find the Delete key. I still reply to the ones that sound sincere, but delete all the others, especially the ones who use strange pseudonyms or do not bother to sign their names at all. You would be amazed at the number of e-mails I receive that say things like "How do you astral travel?" or "Is feng shui real?" These are usually unsigned and come from an anonymous ISP, such as Hotmail. These go straight into the recycle bin.

If you write books on just one subject area, you might be able to write a generic reply that you can send to everyone, with possibly a single sentence at the end to answer their specific question. I write books on all sorts of subjects, which means a generic reply is not possible.

| FREE TALKS

There are many organizations in your community who regularly need guest speakers for their meetings. Most of these groups cannot afford to pay you a fee, but will allow you to sell your books after the talk. You will not make a fortune doing this, but will receive many free meals, meet large numbers of pleasant people, and have a chance to promote yourself and your work in your area.

I live in a city of just over a million people. If I wanted to, I could be speaking at one of these meetings every night of the week. Nowadays, I am selective, but at one time I accepted every invitation that came my way.

It is a simple matter to become a guest speaker. Prepare a thirty-minute talk on the subject of your book. Make sure that it is an introductory talk, and inject as much humor into it as possible. I always memorize the first few sentences of my talks. This means I know exactly what I am going to say when I first stand up to speak. Once I have made this introduction, I am into the talk and can continue without any worries or concerns.

Prepare a handout to give to everyone. This could be a flyer advertising your book and other services. I try to give something that will be kept. Consequently, I always prepare flyers that contain useful hints and suggestions, as well as advertising my book. When I speak on palmistry, for instance, everyone gets a handout that shows the main lines on the palm, and a few words explaining the meaning of each one. My flyer for talks on feng shui lists ten things people can do to improve the feng shui of their home.

Tell people that you are interested in speaking, and word of mouth will probably be enough to get you started. If not, ask around for people to contact at various service and social clubs. Phone them and tell them what you can offer. Most of these groups find it hard to obtain speakers, and will welcome you with open arms. As long as you provide an informative and entertaining speech, the word will get around and organizations will start calling you to book your services.

If people enjoy your talk, they will want to take part of you home in the form of a book. Make this as easy as possible. I accept cash, checks, credit cards, and even let people take books and send the money to me later, if they do not have the money with them. In the last twenty years, I have been let down only once.

You may find that you enjoy giving talks like these. Once you have been doing them for a while, you should consider charging for your services, so that you make money regardless of whether or not people buy your books. I do a mixture of paid and free talks. I charge whenever possible, but realize that many groups can not afford to pay a fee, and continue to talk to them free of charge.

Libraries and schools are also good places in which to give free talks. You may not be able to sell books at these places, but they provide a supportive environment in which to hone your skills at speaking, and provide another way of getting known in your community.

You might consider giving free talks to the general public. You can organize these on your own, or in conjunction with a local bookstore. Radio stations and community newspapers are usually happy to tell their audience about free seminars and workshops. One author I know did very well offering workshops on his subject. The workshop was free, but to get in you had to be holding a copy of his book. I feel it is better to have no restrictions on who can attend, and to have books available for purchase at the back of the room. I try to do these in association with a bookstore, so that they manage the book table and sell the books. My daughter has managed the book table and sold books at public talks where I was unable to interest bookstores in participating.

| Seminars and Workshops

Seminars and workshops vary in length from one hour to two days. They are designed to stand on their own, and need to be promoted well to be viable. Sometimes you will be able to promote the event in conjunction with a New Age store, but more often you will have to take all of the risk yourself. People pay to attend the workshop, and you also have a display of books for sale at the back of the room.

Some people do extremely well with their seminars and workshops. I have had mixed success. Some have been enormously successful and lucrative, while others, promoted in exactly the same way, have lost money. That is why I prefer to let other people handle the promotional aspects of the workshop, while my contribution is to conduct the seminar.

I have done a few workshops with other authors. They worked well, and I would recommend this approach. They are far less stressful than doing them entirely on your own. You can relax while the other authors are talking, and you will probably attract a larger audience, also, because some people will come to hear one author, but will stay to hear them all. Doing events with other authors provides company on the road, as well, which is another positive aspect.

| TEACHING

Adult education classes are booming, and it is not hard to sell yourself as an instructor in your area of expertise. You will not be paid much, but will have the opportunity to introduce your book to your students. You need to ensure that your name, and the name of your book, are included in all of the advertising promoting the classes the school is offering.

| TRUNK SALES

You should have books with you everywhere you go. You never know when the subject of your book will come up, and it is helpful to have copies to sell there and then. I always have a selection of books in the trunk of my car, and over the course of a year sell a surprising number this way. I don't sell books every day, or even every week, but every now and again I sell a few. It all adds up.

I have a personalized license plate for my car (I WRITE). This has brought in many sales over the last few years. Frequently, when I park the car somewhere, someone will ask me what I write. All I need do is open up the trunk, and I have a display of books to offer.

One year, just a few weeks before Christmas, I sold all of the books in the trunk of my car while parked in the parking lot of a shopping mall. I was showing the books to one person, and then someone else expressed interest. Before I knew it, I was surrounded by people wanting to buy books. It was a wonderful experience, and I considered trying to repeat it. I haven't, because I would rather sell my books through the bookstores, as I want them to support me in the future. If I owned a bookstore, I wouldn't be happy to see an author selling his books in the parking lot.

| Direct Mail

You can start a letter-writing campaign to tell everyone you know about your book. Start with friends and acquaintances, and then expand the list to include people you deal with, bookstores, local media, talk show hosts, and radio and TV stations. You can even rent mailing lists, if you wish to mount a larger campaign. With the mail merge capabilities of computers, you can personalize every letter you send out.

A useful extra way to publicize your book is to enclose a small flyer every time you pay an account by mail. Every flyer will be read, and will generate extra sales for you.

| Local Media

Once you are a published author you become a minor celebrity in your neighborhood. You should tell the local media of your success, and this will result in a series of articles and interviews. Keep your local media informed about everything you do. If your book goes into a second printing, for instance, tell the local media. Community newspapers, in particular, are constantly looking for local interest stories, and if you can provide them with interesting information that they can use, they will publish it almost every time.

Shortly before Halloween is a good time to approach your local media with an idea for an interesting story. This need not necessarily be about you and your books. One year I gave our local free newspaper a list of ten interesting facts about Halloween. They published this, and underneath it said that the facts had been contributed by a local author who had written a number of books, including the one I was promoting at the time.

| Magazine and Newspaper Articles

You are a writer. Consequently, it should be a simple matter for you to write a few articles to promote and publicize your book. Naturally, it would be perfect if you could have these published in a magazine that paid you for the contribution, but that is not important if the article is intended to promote your latest book.

Llewellyn publishes their own magazine, *New Worlds*, which promotes new and forthcoming titles. If your book was published by them, the chances are high that an article of seven or eight hundred words about your book would be published here.

An often overlooked market for free articles are bookstore newsletters, such as *Inside Borders*. They include author interviews, as well as brief articles about different new and interesting books.

There are many other places who would publish these articles. New Age newspapers and magazines are the logical ones. However, you might be able to interest your local giveaway paper in a series of articles, just as long as they were not too obviously an advertising exercise.

Naturally, you can write articles on any subject that interests you and submit these to New Age magazines. Leading New Age magazines, such as *FATE*, pay for their submissions, and also include a three- or four-line biography at the end of the article that can promote your book. Do your homework first before submitting articles to magazines. Study recent issues of the magazine, and read the guidelines before sending anything to them. Magazine publishers are always receiving articles that are not right for their needs. (See chapter fifteen for more information on writing articles.)

| BOOK REVIEWS

Your publisher will send out review copies of your book to magazines and newsletters who they think will review your book honestly and fairly. In addition, you can send out review copies to media in your area, if you wish. Remember that not everyone is receptive to the New Age, and you may receive bad reviews because of this.

Some years ago, I sent a review copy of *Feng Shui for Beginners* to our city newspaper. They have a good book review page every Saturday, and I thought it was about time a book of mine was reviewed there. A number of my friends had commented that they never saw my books reviewed anywhere. To my surprise, the review of my book took up half a page and included a full-color illustration of the book's cover. Unfortunately, though, the reviewer had obviously not read the book, and used it as an opportunity to attack the New Age. The article was well written, and made me laugh out loud, but my wife was upset by it, and none of my friends ever mentioned it. However, a strange thing happened as a direct result of this "review." The biggest book chain in New Zealand placed a large order, and has continued to sell the book ever since. They have now sold more than 2,000 copies of this book, and I could not be more grateful for the negative review.

Consequently, there is no need to worry about bad reviews. People usually do not remember them anyway, but will remember hearing the name of the book when they see it in a bookstore. Writers are notoriously thin-skinned, and negative reviews are likely to upset you, especially when they are unfair or biased. Just remember that any mention in the media is good, as long as the title of the book and your name is mentioned.

| AMAZON READERS REVIEWS

There is one exception to this. These are readers' comments about books on Amazon.com, and other Internet sites. My first experience of these occurred several years ago, when I gave a talk about one of my books at a bookstore. After the talk, someone in the store, who had not listened to my talk, came over and made some extremely rude remarks about me, my book, and the New Age. I remained pleasant and polite. After all, I was in a bookstore doing an event. Eventually, the man left, telling me as he went that he would put a bad review of my book on Amazon.com.

Sure enough, a week or two later, a negative review appeared from someone who was not brave enough to use his own name, and also used an anonymous Hotmail address. In his review, he said that he had not read the book, but had flipped through it in a bookstore. I immediately wrote to Amazon.com, telling them the story, and also complaining that the man had not even read the book. Amazon.com replied saying they felt it was a legitimate review, and that it would stay.

I like the idea that readers can post their own reviews of books they have read. However, I don't like the fact that negative reviews can be posted anonymously, as this allows people who perhaps do not like you, or simply don't like the New Age, to vent their spleen at your expense.

A few years ago, I spent an evening with a reasonably well-known English New Age author. After several glasses of Scotch he told me that he regularly posted negative reviews of books written by other authors on the subjects that he wrote on.

Another author I met (not in the New Age) told me that he pays his grandchildren to write positive reviews of his books. Consequently, I never look at the reviews of my books on Amazon.com, nor do I read the reviews of books that I am planning to buy. The idea of on-line reviews is wonderful. I just wish the system was not so easy to manipulate.

| Book Launch Parties

I have never had a book launch party. However, I have attended a huge number of them, and know many authors who have had them. It would be unusual for a New Age publisher to put on a book launch party for you, so if you want one, you will have to do it yourself.

Bear in mind that you will probably not recoup the costs involved. However, you might be able to get some local publicity from it, and it is a good opportunity for a party. Make sure that you have at least enough books for everyone present to buy one. Have one or two people responsible for handling the sales. This means that you are not directly involved with the business of selling books, and are free to work the room and autograph books.

You will have to make a speech. Be modest, entertaining, and brief. I have attended far too many book launches where the author went on interminably, telling us in enormous detail every stage of the writing process. People are at your book launch to have fun, see friends, meet people, and ideally, to buy a book. Make sure they have a good time by keeping the speeches to a minimum.

Afterward, think about the good time you had. Don't think about the people who drank all your wine and did not buy a book, or the people who promised to come but failed to turn up. As you can see, I do not recommend book launch parties. If you regard it as a party, you'll have fun, but don't consider it seriously as a way to promote your book. There are much better ways of doing that.

| CAPITALIZING ON THE NEWS

You might be able to attach your book to something that is going on in the news. If anything happens that relates, even tenuously, to the subject of your book, contact the media and be prepared to talk about it.

To do this effectively, you will need to have a press kit ready. Your publisher will provide you with these. They are expensive to produce, so it is important that you use them. They are of no use to anyone if they are left on a shelf.

| BOOK TOUR

A book tour is when an author travels to several cities to promote his or her latest book. It is unusual for an author to have a book tour to promote a first book, as tours are extremely expensive in both time and money. Also, not every book lends itself to a book tour. Your publicist will need to organize radio and television interviews to help promote your book signings and other events. He or she will prepare a press kit and then spend countless hours on the phone speaking to the media, telling them what you can do for their program. It is hard, time-consuming work. Your publicist has to remain constantly aware of every angle to get the media interested in you. Travel arrangements and hotel bookings will also have to be made.

Pack lightly for the tour. I take one suitcase and a briefcase that I carry on to the plane with me. I can handle these on my own, without requiring assistance. I usually take a travel alarm clock as a backup, because I am not a natural early riser (however, with increased airport security, this may be no longer practical). I no longer carry a laptop computer with me. Originally, I thought I'd be able to do some writing on the road. However, I soon learned that I was too tired in my off periods to write, and my time was better spent relaxing and getting ready for the next event. Also, while on tour, you need to be totally focused on the book you are promoting. Consequently, it is hard to actively write one book while busy promoting another.

Finally, you are on tour. You need to be physically fit, and ready to do early morning breakfast shows as well as late evening workshops and talks. You will have to eat as, and when, you can. I hate eating late at night and then going straight to bed, but this is a common occurrence on a book tour. A book tour is exhausting, both mentally and physically, but it can sell a large number of books.

Like most authors, there will be moments when you wonder if it is worth putting all the time and effort into promoting and publicizing your book. If only two people turn up at your book signing, and someone writes negative things about your book on the Internet, you may feel like retreating and giving up the whole business. That is fine if you intend writing only one book. However, if you are in this business for the long term, you need to get known, you need to be visible, and you need to promote, promote, promote.

14

NEW AGE FICTION

We hear a great deal about successful fiction in the media. Some novels sell hundreds of thousands of copies, and the film rights sell for huge amounts. It is easy to forget that many more nonfiction books are published every year than fiction. Nonfiction books are easier to sell to a publisher than fiction, and they also tend to stay in print longer.

However, despite that, many would-be authors want to write fiction. I enjoy writing fiction, but make the bulk of my income from my nonfiction books. Consequently, it is better for me to spend most of my time writing nonfiction. This is a business decision on my part. I have a family to support and need to put most of my time into income-producing activities. However, I intend writing more fiction as and when I can.

New Age fiction covers a wide field. Hermann Hesse and J. D. Salinger would not describe themselves as New Age writers, but some of their work fits into that category. Many fantasy novels, for instance, could loosely be described as New Age fiction. The numerous books on the Arthurian tradition and the Holy Grail fit into this category. I have read New Age–type crime novels where the detective is able to use his or her remote viewing talent, or other psychic skills, to catch the murderer. Books of this sort are usually published by mainstream publishers, rather than specialist New Age publishers.

An excellent example of a New Age novel that was published by a mainstream publisher is *Ferney* by James Long.[1] You should study this book if you are interested in writing New Age fiction, as it is a perfect example of how the New Age theme (reincarnation in this case) is an integral part of the whole book. *Ferney* is a story of soul mates who have been together in many previous lifetimes. One partner remembers them all, and gradually encourages his soul mate to discover for herself the fascinating stories of their previous incarnations. James Long usually writes thrillers, but I hope he will write more New Age fiction in the future.

| FICTION REQUIREMENTS

New Age publishers want their fiction to contain more than an exciting story. Llewellyn, for instance, wants their New Age fiction to be educational as well as entertaining. The topics should reflect "true 'occult' principles: astrology, parapsychology, Witchcraft/Wicca, Pagan lifestyles." They publish no supernatural horror.

Consequently, you need to learn your publisher's requirements before starting to write your New Age novel. Study the guidelines, and read several New Age novels that your prospective publisher has already published. The primary rule still applies: give your publishers what they want.

If I were to write a novel for Llewellyn I would try to immerse believable characters into a fast-moving, exciting story. The occult material would be an integral part of the plot. For instance, at some stage the hero might perform a spell or ritual. I would provide enough information to enable the readers to reenact the ritual if they wished. If one of the characters was an astrologer, he or she would impart practical information about astrology in the course of the book. Your readers will not want to have the plot held up while you expound at great length on different methods of crystal gazing, for instance, but they will enjoy learning interesting facts painlessly while reading an absorbing story.

The occult elements cannot be added later to give the book a New Age slant. They must be an integral part of the plot. It is a good idea to decide on what aspects of the psychic world will be covered in your book before thinking about anything else. Once you have that clearly in mind, allow the characters and the story to evolve from this, and you will write a true New Age novel.

| FICTION OR NONFICTION?

Before writing a novel, ask yourself if the occult knowledge you are going to include might not be better taught in a work of nonfiction. Some years ago, I read that mirrors were popular tools for psychic development in the Victorian era. My first thought was that I could write a story involving someone alive today who found a psychic mirror that had belonged to her great grandmother. I imagined that with practice, she found she could communicate with her long-dead great grandmother using the mirror. I became fascinated with psychic mirrors and carried on with my research. What I learned was astounding. There is a wealth of information about psychic mirrors that is not commonly known today. I now have several notebooks and a file box full of information on this subject.

Consequently, if I was going to write about psychic mirrors, I would probably choose to write a nonfiction book on the subject, rather than fiction. It would be more enjoyable to write a novel using the mirror, but I would be able to include much more useful information in a work of nonfiction.

The techniques of fiction are different to those of nonfiction. If you intend writing fiction of any sort, you should read as many novels as possible, and also study some of the many books available on the art of writing fiction.[2]

If you are going to write a work of popular fiction, all the standard rules of novel writing apply. You need a good plot, interesting characters, conflict, and an eventual, logical resolution. Your readers must be willing to suspend their natural disbelief and enjoy the story. Only afterward should they realize that they have learned valuable information from your book.

| TEENAGE FICTION

There is a growing interest in New Age novels for the teenage market, as well. In the 1990s, Christopher Pike introduced many young readers to different aspects of the occult in a series of exciting books. Today, Silver RavenWolf is introducing teenagers to Wicca with her series of popular books. Young people are keen to learn all they can about the New Age. If you enjoy dealing with young people, and can talk to them at their level, you might consider writing for the teenage market.

Some people think that writing juvenile books is easy. It is not. It is at least as difficult as writing books for adults, and probably harder. You need to get your voice exactly right, be up-to-date with the interests of contemporary teenagers, and be able to write a fast-moving, exciting story. It is a hard market to crack, but a rewarding one if you are good at it.

| LONGEVITY

Writing New Age fiction is a difficult art to master, but if you are successful your novels will have a long life. *Séraphîta* by Honoré de Balzac (1799–1850) is arguably the greatest occult novel ever written. It explains valuable Rosicrucian secrets, and reveals the unlimited spiritual potential latent inside all of us. It was published in 1835 and is still being read today. Maria Corelli (1855–1924) wrote twenty-eight novels that were enormously popular in her lifetime, and some of them are still being sold today. Her first book, *A Romance of Two Worlds*, was written when she was only twenty-two, although it was not published until 1886. It retells her own psychic experiences in the form of a novel. Aleister Crowley's (1875–1947) New Age novel, *The Moonchild*, is still being read today. Dion Fortune wrote both fiction and nonfiction. Her novels, *The Demon Lover* (London: Noel Douglas, 1927), *The Sea Priestess* (London: Aquarian Press, 1957), *Moon Magic* (London: Aquarian Press, 1956), *The Goat-Foot God* (London: Williams & Norgate, Ltd., 1936), and *The Winged Bull* (London: Williams & Norgate, Ltd., 1935) are still in print, and still well worth reading, sixty years after she wrote them. Charles Williams wrote a series of superb novels that incorporate spirituality and the New Age. *The Greater Trumps* (London, Victor Gollancz, Ltd., 1933) is my favorite, and provides a huge amount of information about the major arcana of the tarot deck in a fascinating, intricate story. His other New Age novels are: *All Hallow's Eve* (London: Faber & Faber, Ltd., 1945), *Descent into Hell* (New York: Pellegrini & Cudahy, 1949), *Many Dimensions* (London: Victor Gollancz, Ltd., 1931), *The Place of the Lion* (London: Victor Gollancz, Ltd., 1931), and *War in Heaven* (London: Victor Gollancz, Ltd., 1930).

... You want your readers to enjoy the book while also learning interesting and practical occult information ...

Joan Grant wrote a series of books that were published as historical novels, although, in reality, they were her memories of her previous lives. Her autobiography, *Far Memory*, explains how she became aware of her ability to recall her past lives in vivid detail.

T. Lobsang Rampa (the pseudonym of Cyril Hoskin) introduced many people to the psychic world with a series of books, beginning with *The Third Eye*, published in 1956 (London: Secker & Warburg, Ltd.). Although they were ostensibly nonfiction, describing his experiences as a Tibetan lama, I would classify them as New Age novels.

You will find it worthwhile to study these classic New Age novels, as well as some of the contemporary ones, before starting to write one yourself.

15

WRITING
ARTICLES

There is a steady demand for articles on New Age topics, not only from New Age magazines, but also from many general interest publications. Unfortunately, these markets do not pay well, so I would not recommend that you write articles for monetary reasons alone.

However, articles can be useful for a number of reasons. You can write articles to:

- Practice and hone your writing skills.

- Start your writing career with projects that can be completed quickly.

- Help promote your books.

- Create interest in the topics you write about.

- Build up a following of people who are interested in your work.

- Determine what interest there is in specific topics.

- Gain regular income from a monthly column.

- Publish information on topics that do not warrant a full-length book.

- Have your work published quickly.

I have already mentioned how writing articles can help you develop your writing skills. This does not mean that you can quickly dash off an article and send it off. Everything you write needs to be the very best you are capable of producing. Your articles need to be researched, outlined and well written.

Articles are a highly effective way to advertise and promote your books or anything else you might be doing, such as seminars and workshops. People who enjoy your articles will seek out your books and events in which you are involved. The benefits of this frequently outweigh the fee you will receive for the article.

Articles also help create interest in the topics that you enjoy writing about. If you have specialized knowledge about a little-known aspect of the New Age, you can help create a larger audience for this topic by writing articles about it before starting to write a book. In fact, you can write articles while you are researching the book. By the time you have written several articles on the subject, you will be considered an authority, making it easier to find a publisher for the finished book.

If you write articles regularly, you will gradually build up a loyal following of readers who will be looking for everything you write. This will help the sales of your books.

| MARKET RESEARCH

You can use your articles to help determine the degree of interest in the different subjects you write about. If a particular article receives a great deal of favorable feedback from your readers, it might be worth writing a book on the subject. An example of this is an article called "Psychic Animals" that I wrote for the May 2000 issue of *FATE* magazine. As a result of the feedback I received from this article, I wrote a book called *Is Your Pet Psychic?* (Llewellyn, 2002) the positive feedback, it is doubtful that I would have ever written a book on that particular subject.

| A Regular Column

Writing magazine articles is not particularly lucrative, but a monthly column provides you with a regular pay check every month. For ten years I wrote a monthly column for *Vibrations*. I was able to write about anything in the psychic world that attracted my attention. It gave me a chance to explore and write about all sorts of things that interested me, excited me, angered me, and fascinated me. I made observations about different things I did or saw. In one sense, the column was like a diary in which I recorded snippets of my life. And yes, some of the columns created enough interest to inspire me to write books about them.

You need to be able to keep to rigid deadlines if you take on a weekly or monthly column. I was able to do this by always having two or three articles in reserve. This meant that the articles kept appearing, even when I was away from home for lengthy periods. However, this is not always possible. If your regular column is about upcoming events in your local community, for instance, you would not be able to write your column months ahead of publication date. Make sure that impending deadlines do not place too much pressure on you before agreeing to a regular commitment.

| Preliminary Research

Every now and again you'll chance upon a fascinating topic. You might want to write a book about it, but not have enough information to do so. The answer is to turn it into a magazine article. This allows the information to be published and made available to others. The response you receive from the article will also tell you if the subject is worth researching further. However, if you are like me, you will probably research it anyway, purely from an interest point of view.

| WHAT ARTICLES TO WRITE

The most publishable New Age books are "how-to" titles. However, your articles need not be limited in this way. These are the most popular types of articles:

How-To—Articles teaching readers how to do anything are always saleable. Naturally, you can not go into great depth in an article, but you should still provide enough practical information to allow the reader to practice whatever it is you are teaching. It is a good idea to ask people who have no knowledge of the subject to read your article and see if they can follow your instructions.

Interview—In an interview article you talk with a well-known or knowledgeable person and write an article based on it. This type of article may simply consist of questions and answers, or alternatively—and usually better—you could write a profile of the person, in which case the questions and answers provide the raw material that you use as the starting point of your article.

Historical—The New Age has a fascinating history, and there is a need for articles about little-known aspects of it. I would love to read more about the Hermetic Brotherhood of Luxor, for instance. If you can uncover new information, you will find a ready market for your findings.

Personal Experience—Articles that relate how you became interested in the psychic world, had a near-death experience, or developed the ability to see auras are always popular. However, this is not an opportunity for an ego trip. You will find greater success with this type of article if you remain modest, and write about your failures as well as your successes.

Travel—There are many mystical and holy places around the world. Your visit to Glastonbury Abbey would be saleable if it contained useful information or had an unusual slant to it. You do not need to travel around the world to find interesting places, either. You could write a fascinating article about a nearby haunted house, for instance.

Open-minded Investigative—These articles are hard to write, as you need to steer a path between being skeptical and overly credulous. To use the haunted house scenario again, you could write it from an investigative point of view, trying to determine the reality of the phenomena that is occurring in the house.

InspirationaL—The purpose of an inspirational article is to motivate and inspire the reader. An example would be a variation of the personal experience article in which you explain how you succeeded at something, and tell the reader that as you were able to do it, he or she can too. Naturally, an inspirational article needs to be positive and uplifting, and must convince the reader that he or she can achieve success.

Questionnaires—These articles consist of a simple questionnaire that the readers can take to determine their ability or aptitude at a certain activity. Articles such as "Test Your Psychic Ability" fall into this category. Your readers answer a series of questions, and then add up their scores to see what natural ability they possess.

Market Research—In this type of article you ask the readers for feedback. This could be done for a variety of reasons. If you are writing a book on past life memories, you might want to find out the percentage of readers who have already experienced a past life regression. You might want to find out how many readers believe in astral travel or the healing power of bee pollen.

Research of this sort is valuable to determine the potential demand for a book you might be thinking about writing. It can also provide you with facts and figures to include in the book.

Writing articles is like writing books in miniature. You still need to come up with a topic, research it, decide on a suitable publisher, come up with a good title, outline it, and then write it. You then have to send it to the magazine you think would like it, and risk rejection. You might be asked to rewrite the article one or more times before they buy it. If you are fortunate, the magazine will pay you on acceptance, which means you receive payment immediately. It is more likely that the magazine will pay you after the article has been published. This will probably be several months after you wrote it. When the magazine comes out people will read your article, but it is likely to be forgotten as soon as the next issue appears. Unlike books, magazine articles are ephemeral.

| SPECIALISTS AND GENERALISTS

Some writers specialize in just one subject, while others write about anything that attracts their interest. There are advantages and disadvantages with both approaches. Specialists write about a subject that they are passionate about. They look at their subject from every possible point of view, and write articles about their findings. Specialists become known as authorities in their subject area, and if an editor is looking for an article (or a book) on that topic, he or she would think of the specialist first.

Generalists write about a wide range of subjects. They are versatile people who enjoy the variety this approach provides. Most newspaper reporters are generalists. They might write about problems in a nuclear power plant one day, rising unemployment the next, and a murder trial the day after. Obviously, they need to be good researchers and interviewers to find the facts they need. However, they can often find a fresh angle or approach that specialists might overlook.

The best approach is to write what you enjoy writing about. If you are totally absorbed in dream interpretation, for example, and enjoy sharing your findings with others, you should consider specializing in this field. However, if you are also interested in auras, crystals, levitation, Eastern religions, and ghosts, you would probably have more satisfaction writing about all of your various interests.

I am definitely a generalist. You might put this down to my Sagittarius sun and Gemini moon, or perhaps my five Life Path in numerology. Whatever it is, I am always involved in a huge range of subjects, and want to share what I learn with others. This is one reason why I write articles as well as books.

You need to decide what subjects you want to write about. What do you enjoy reading? What are your hobbies and talents? What are you good at? Answering these questions will determine whether you are a specialist or a generalist. You can even be a bit of both, writing about your specialty interest whenever possible, but also writing articles on other subjects from time to time.

| IDEAS FOR ARTICLES

As a writer, you probably don't need to be told that ideas for magazine articles are all around you. Most of my ideas come from talking with people and asking them questions. Other people's articles also provide ideas. I might read an article and, at the end of it, have a question that the writer failed to answer. Searching for the answer elsewhere often gives me enough material for an article of my own. Something I hear on the radio or television might trigger an idea for an article. Speaking with people after a talk or workshop is another excellent source of article ideas.

Of course, once you have an idea, you have to choose the right magazine for which to write. Is it an idea they would be receptive to? Are you interested enough in the topic to do the necessary research? Will you make enough money from the article to justify the amount of time it will take to research and write? These questions have to be answered before you sit down to write.

| REWARDS

Is it worth it? I still write several articles a year, so obviously consider them worth doing. However, the only reason I continue writing them is because they provide yet another way for me to promote my books. Your motivations are probably different than mine. Here are the six main reasons why you should consider writing articles, as well as books.

1. Writing articles is an excellent way to develop the habit of writing. This is a discipline that often needs to be developed. It is much less threatening to write a two thousand-word article than a sixty thousand-word book.

2. The more writing you do, the better you will become. Consequently, writing articles will help you learn the craft.

3. Writing articles will help you to build up your name and reputation. This is useful if you are working in the New Age field as a practitioner of some sort, or if you are writing, or planning to write, New Age books.

4. Articles provide an opportunity to determine the degree of interest in a particular subject.

5. Writing books is a lengthy task that can take months or years. It can be relaxing to sit down and write about something completely different. It is also extremely pleasant to start and finish a writing project in a matter of hours.

6. Articles can help your cash flow. Writers of books receive their royalties every six months. It is not much fun when sudden expenses arise, and your next royalty check is two or three months away. Writing articles is a pleasant way to earn some

extra money, and promote your other activities at the same time.

| How To Start

Choose the magazine you would like to write for. Ideally, this is a magazine that you already subscribe to, or read on a regular basis. Study as many recent issues as you can. This basic market research is essential. It will tell you the type of article they publish, and the length of article they prefer. It will also give you some idea as to the magazine's approach and style. Look up the magazine in the latest edition of *Writer's Market* to see if the magazine provides writer's guidelines. You can frequently download the guidelines over the Internet. Make sure that you study them carefully before writing your article.

Writer's Market will also provide you with the pay rates, tell you how much of the magazine is written by freelancers, and if you should query the editor first, or send in the finished article. It also includes the editor's name. Make sure that you always use the latest edition of *Writer's Market*, and check the editor's name in the current edition of the magazine, just in case the editorship has changed.

Many magazines prefer to receive a query letter rather than the completed article. This is a useful protection for you as well. For instance, your article will be rejected if the magazine has recently bought an article on a similar topic to yours. The editor might like your idea for an article, but have definite ideas on how you should approach it.

Your query letter is your sales pitch to the editor. It should look professional and be addressed to him or her by name. Make sure you spell the editor's name correctly. My brother-in-law's surname is Laery. He—quite rightly—hates receiving letters that misspell his name as Leary. What faith will an editor have in you if you do not even check the spelling of his or her name?

I prefer to write a brief cover letter and enclose a separate article proposal. Some writers incorporate both together. There is no perfect length for an outline. It needs to be long enough to tell the editor exactly what you are going to include in your article, and no longer.

You need an intriguing title. Visualize your title printed in large letters on the front cover of the magazine. Is it intriguing enough to entice potential readers to pick the magazine up?

Begin your outline with the paragraph you intend starting the article with. Follow this with a comprehensive account of what the article will be about. You can not say that the article will be about feng shui, for instance. That is far too broad a subject to cover in a short article. However, you might write an article on feng shui in the garden, or the office, or for relationships. Be as specific as possible.

... visualize your title printed in large letters on the front cover of the magazine ...

Finish the proposal with information about yourself. Naturally, include any relevant writing credentials you may have. Conversely, do not mention your lack of experience if this is, for instance, your first article proposal. Explain why you are the perfect person to write this particular article.

Finally, send your proposal to the editor. You might have to wait a few months for a reply. Do not stop here, though. Come up with other proposals and send them out as well. This means that you will not be devastated if your first proposal is turned down, because you will have other proposals out there as well. This is known as "keeping the pipeline full."

It is a waste of time asking an editor why he or she turned down your proposal. It could be for any number of reasons that are unrelated to your writing ability. The editor may have a large supply of accepted articles, and is not accepting anything new at the moment. He or she may have accepted, or published, something similar to your proposal recently. You may not have done your homework properly, and sent your proposal to the wrong magazine. Be grateful that you did not write the entire article, and send the proposal to another editor.

If the article is a short one, it is better to write it and send it in on speculation, rather than querying the editor first. This is because it would take you just as long to write the article as it would the proposal, and it is a better use of your time to write the article.

If your article is aimed at a certain time of year, such as Halloween, make your proposal eight or nine months ahead of time. This will put you ahead of any other authors who might be thinking of similar articles.

Become a professional. Make sure that your manuscripts are the very best that you are capable of producing. They need to be consistently well written and well presented. Stick to any deadlines. Study your markets, and constantly look for new and alternative markets for your articles. Keep track of your submissions. I have an exercise book in which I list every book and article I write. I keep a record of the publishers I sent them to, the dates on which they were posted, and the responses.

Work hard, but take time off to relax. Enjoy your article writing, but keep searching for book-length ideas. You will never make a living writing articles, but—ultimately—you will be able to make a living with your books.

Conclusion

The New Age field is becoming increasingly mainstream. New Age books are no longer hidden away in the occult section of the bookstore. Because this field is growing rapidly, there are numerous opportunities for motivated, industrious, and ambitious writers.

The fact that you have read this far indicates that you are serious about becoming a New Age author. No matter where in your writing career you may be at present, you have the potential to become successful in this field. Like everything else, though, there is a price to be paid. Here are some questions that will help you discover how serious you are about becoming a new age author.

1. Are you prepared to do whatever is necessary to improve your writing skills?

2. Do you have knowledge that you want to share with others? If not, are you prepared to study and research until you reach this position?

3. Are you prepared to spend months, and possibly even years, working at your manuscript with no guarantee of publication when it is finished?

4. Are you willing to accept the possible rejection of your manuscript?

5. Are you prepared to write another book if your first book proves unpublishable?

6. Are you prepared to make the changes to your manuscript that a potential publisher considers necessary?

7. Are you disciplined enough to keep working at your manuscript until it is finished?

If you can honestly answer yes to all of these questions, you have the potential to be successful in this fascinating, exciting, growing field. I wish you enormous success and look forward to seeing your books in my local bookstore.

NOTES

Introduction

1. NORC survey reported in *American Health*, January–February 1987. Also in Robert C. Cowen's "Research Notebook" column in *Christian Science Monitor*, July 7, 1987.

2. A browse through *Writer's Market* will give you some idea of the numbers of books that are published by first-time New Age authors. At Celestial Arts, 30 percent of their books are from first-time authors. At Crossing Press it is 10 percent, Hampton Roads 50 percent, Hay House 10 percent, Inner Traditions 10 percent, Llewellyn 30 percent, Quest Books 50 percent, and Samuel Weiser 50 percent.

3. Richard Webster, *Secrets of Ghost Writing* (London, UK: Breese Books Limited, 1987).

Chapter One

1. Jerrold R. Jenkins with Mardi Link, *Inside the Bestsellers* (Traverse City, Mich.: Traverse and Easton, 1997), 163–164.

2. Richard Webster, *In the Palm of Your Hand* (Albuquerque, N.M.: Flora and Company, 1993).

3. Jerrold R. Jenkins with Mardi Link, *Inside the Bestsellers*, 42.

4. Francis L. and Roberta B. Fugate, *Secrets of the World's Best-Selling Writer: The Storytelling Techniques of Erle Stanley Gardner* (New York, N.Y.: William Morrow and Company, Inc., 1980), 13.

5. These percentages are taken from the publishers' entries in *Writer's Market*.

Chapter Two

1. Erle Stanley Gardner, quoted in *Secrets of the World's Best-Selling Writer: The Storytelling Techniques of Erle Stanley Gardner* by Francis L. and Roberta B. Fugate, 35.

2. John Milton Edwards (a pseudonym of William Wallace Cook), *The Fiction Factory* (Ridgewood, N.J.: The Editor Company, 1912).

3. Jack London did write one book that could be considered New Age. This was *The Star Rover*, a novel with an astral travel theme.

4. Francis L. and Roberta B. Fugate, *Secrets of the World's Best-Selling Writer*, 123.

Chapter Three

1. Robert Louis Stevenson, quoted in *Writing with Precision* by Jefferson D. Bates (Washington, D.C.: Acropolis Books Limited, revised edition, 1985), xv.

Chapter Six

1. There are an increasing number of books that give advice on researching on the Internet. Look for the most recent ones. Here are some suggested titles to get you started: *Find It Online: The Complete Guide to Online Research* by Alan M. Schlein (Facts on Demand), *Cybersearch: Research Techniques in the Electronic Age* by John A. Butler (Penguin Books), *Find It Fast: How to Uncover Expert Information on any Subject Online or in Print* by Robert I. Berkman (Harper Resource), and *Super Searchers in the News: The Online Secrets of Journalists and News Researchers* by Paula J. Hane (Cyberage Books).

Chapter Eight

1. Ken Ring, *How to Make a Stone Circle* (Auckland, New Zealand: Milton Press, 2001).

2. Joel Saltzman, *If You Can Talk, You Can Write* (New York: Warner Books, Inc., 1993), 89.

Chapter Ten

1. Bill Henderson and André Bernard, editors. *Pushcart's Complete Rotten Reviews and Rejections* (Wainscott, N.Y.: Pushcard Press, 1998).

2. Bill Henderson and André Bernard, editors. *Pushcart's Complete Rotten Reviews and Rejections*, 206.

Chapter Eleven

1. Brad Bunnin and Peter Beren, *The Writer's Legal Companion* (Reading, Mass.: Addison-Wesley, 1988).

2. Mark L. Levine, *Negotiating a Book Contract: A Guide for Authors, Agents, and Lawyers* (Mt. Kisko, N.Y.: Moyer Bell, Limited, 1988).

Chapter Fourteen

1. James Long, *Ferney* (New York: HarperCollins Publishers, 1998).

2. Two books that have been useful for me in writing commercial fiction are: *Writing the Breakout Novel: Insider Advice for Taking Your Fiction to the Next Level* by Donald Maas (Cincinnati, Ohio: Writer's Digest Books, 2001), and *Writing the Blockbuster Novel* by Albert Zuckerman (Cincinnati, Ohio: Writer's Digest Books, 1994).

SUGGESTED READING

American Society of Journalists and Authors. *The Complete Guide to Writing Non-Fiction*. Ed. Glen Evans. Cincinnati: Writer's Digest Books, 1983.

Appelbaum, Judith. *How to Get Happily Published*. New York: Harper & Row, Inc., 1988.

Balkin, Richard. *How to Understand and Negotiate a Book Contract or Magazine Agreement*. Cincinnati: Writer's Digest Books, 1985.

Bates, Jefferson D. *Writing with Precision*. Washington, D.C.: Acropolis Books Limited, 1978. Revised edition 1985.

Blanco, Jodee. *The Complete Guide to Book Publicity*. New York: Allworth Press, 2000.

Booth, Wayne C., Gregory G. Colomb, and Joseph M. Williams. *The Craft of Research*. Chicago: The University of Chicago Press, 1995.

Bunnin, Brad, and Peter Beren. *The Writer's Legal Companion*. Reading, Mass.: Addison-Wesley, Inc., 1988.

The Chicago Manual of Style. Chicago: University of Chicago Press, 1982.

Clouse, Barbara Fine. *Working It Out: A Trouble-shooting Guide for*

Writers. New York: McGraw-Hill, Inc., 1993.

Curtis, Richard. *How to be Your Own Literary Agent: The Business of Getting Your Book Published.* Boston: Houghton Mifflin, 1984.

Gaughen, Barbara, and Ernest Weckbaugh. *Book Blitz: Getting Your Book in the News.* Burbank, Calif.: Best-seller Books, 1994.

Goldberg, Natalie. *Writing Down the Bones: Freeing the Writer Within.* Boston: Shambhala Publications, 1986.

Gross, Gerald. *Editors on Editing: What Writers Need to Know about What Editors Do.* New York: Grove Press, Inc., 1993.

Henderson, Bill, and André Bernard (editors). *Pushcart's Complete Rotten Reviews and Rejections: A History of Insult, a Solace to Writers.* Wainscott, N.Y: Pushcart Press, 1998.

Herman, Jeff, and Herman, Deborah Levine. *Write the Perfect Book Proposal: 10 Proposals that Sold and Why.* New York: John Wiley & Sons, Inc., second edition, 2001 (originally published in 1993).

Horowitz, Lois. *Knowing Where to Look: The Ultimate Guide to Research.* Cincinnati: Writer's Digest Books, 1984.

Kremer, John. *1001 Ways to Market Your Books—for Authors and Publishers.* Fairfield, Iowa: Ad-Lib Publications, 1986.

Levine, Mark L. *Negotiating a Book Contract: A Guide for Authors, Agents, and Lawyers.* Mt. Kisko, N.Y: Moyer Bell, Limited, 1988.

Literary Market Place. New York: R. R. Bowker, published annually.

Maas, Donald. *Writing the Breakout Novel: Insider Advice for Taking Your Fiction to the Next Level.* Cincinnati: Writer's Digest Books, 2001.

McQuain, Jeffrey. *Power Language: Getting the Most Out of Your Words.* New York: Houghton Mifflin Company, 1996.

Ross, Marilyn and Tom. *Jump Start Your Book Sales: A Money-making Guide for Authors, Independent Publishers and Small Presses.* Buena Vista, Colo.: Communication Creativity, 1999.

Saltzman, Joel. *If You Can Talk, You Can Write.* New York: Warner Books, Inc., 1993.

Strunk, W., Jr., and E. B. White. *The Elements of Style.* New York: Macmillan Publishing Co., Inc., 1959. Third edition, 1979.

Writer's Market. Cincinnati: Writer's Digest Books, published annually.

Zerubavel, Eviatar. *The Clockwork Muse: A Practical Guide to Writing Theses, Dissertations, and Books.* Cambridge, Mass.: Harvard University Press, 1999.

Zinsser, William. *On Writing Well: An Informal Guide to Writing Nonfiction.* New York: Harper and Row, Inc., 1980.

Zuckerman, Albert. *Writing the Blockbuster Novel.* Cincinnati: Writer's Digest Books, 1994.

INDEX

☾ ORDER LLEWELLYN BOOKS TODAY!

Llewellyn publishes hundreds of books on your favorite subjects! To get these exciting books, including the ones on the following pages, check your local bookstore or order them directly from Llewellyn.

Order Online:
Visit our website at www.llewellyn.com, select your books, and order them on our secure server.

Order by Phone:
- Call toll-free within the U.S. at 1-877-NEW-WRLD (1-877-639-9753)
  Call toll-free within Canada at 1-866-NEW-WRLD (1-866-639-9753)
- We accept VISA, MasterCard, and American Express

Order by Mail:
Send the full price of your order (MN residents add 7% sales tax) in U.S. funds, plus postage & handling to:
> **Llewellyn Worldwide**
> **P.O. Box 64383, Dept. 0-7387-0344-3**
> **St. Paul, MN 55164-0383, U.S.A.**

Postage & Handling:
> **Standard** (U.S., Mexico, & Canada). If your order is:
> > Up to $25.00, add $3.50
> > $25.01 - $48.99, add $4.00
> > $49.00 and over, FREE STANDARD SHIPPING
>
> (Continental U.S. orders ship UPS. AK, HI, PR, & P.O. Boxes ship USPS 1st class. Mex. & Can. ship PMB.)

> ### International Orders:
> **Surface Mail:** For orders of $20.00 or less, add $5 plus $1 per item ordered. For orders of $20.01 and over, add $6 plus $1 per item ordered.

> **Air Mail:**
> *Books:* Postage & Handling is equal to the total retail price of all books in the order.
> *Non-book items:* Add $5 for each item.

Orders are processed within 2 business days. Please allow for normal shipping time.
Postage and handling rates subject to change.